AS THE CROW FLIES

MY JOURNEY TO IRONMAN® WORLD CHAMPION

CRAIG
ALEXANDER

AS THE CROW FLIES
MY JOURNEY TO IRONMAN® WORLD CHAMPION

PHOTOGRAPHY BY PAUL K. ROBBINS

VELO press

BOULDER, COLORADO

3002 Sterling Circle, Suite 100
Boulder, Colorado 80301-2338 USA
(303) 440-0601 / Fax (303) 444-6788 / E-mail velopress@competitorgroup.com

Distributed in the United States and Canada by Ingram Publisher Services

Library of Congress Cataloging-in-Publication Data
Alexander, Craig, 1973-
As the crow flies: my journey to ironman world champion / Craig Alexander; photography by Paul K. Robbins.
         p. cm.
ISBN 978-1-934030-94-3 (hardcover: alk. paper)
1. Alexander, Craig, 1973- 2. Triathletes—Australia—Biography. 3. Ironman triathlons. I. Title.
GV1060.73.A43 2012
796.4257092—dc23
[B]
                              2012022373

For information on purchasing VeloPress books, please call (800) 811-4210 ext. 2138 or visit www.velopress.com.

This paper meets the requirements of ANSI/NISO Z39.48-1992 (Permanence of Paper).

Cover design by Vicki Hopewell and Elizabeth Downey
Interior design and composition by Vicki Hopewell
Cover and interior photographs by Paul K. Robbins, except for the photograph on p. 61 by Larry Rosa
and both photographs on p. 153 courtesy of the KIDS Foundation.
Illustration on cloth cover and on p. 189 by Chris Wood, courtesy of Road ID.

Text set in FF Scala and Gotham.

12   13   14 / 10   9   8   7   6   5   4   3   2   1

Always for Neri, Lucy, and Austin // C.A.

For Ludivine, Tom, and Lilou—my love, my life // P.K.R.

Contents

ix / **FOREWORD**
by Greg Welch

xvii / **INTRODUCTION**

1 / **COMMITMENT**
Early-season training

29 / **FOCUS**
A new goal comes into view

43 / **SETBACKS**
Holding it together when things fall apart

67 / **GOING SOLO**
Building up to the world championships

91 / **FINAL COUNTDOWN**
Returning to Kona

137 / **BRINGING IT HOME**
Where it all started

155 / **SUB 8**
The road ahead

173 / **EPILOGUE**

174 / **ACHIEVEMENTS**

180 / **ACKNOWLEDGMENTS**

185 / **ABOUT THE PHOTOGRAPHER**

Foreword

It was late summer 1997 when a group of young and very fast Aussie triathletes gathered on the sunshine coast in Australia as Olympic prospects for the first-ever triathlon in the summer Olympic Games. I was selected to be on the "A" team. Then there was a "B" team, and then there was a development team.

I remember vividly one day when we strolled over to a local high school to use its 400-meter grass oval, which was filled with gopherlike holes that were ready to break our dreams along with our ankles. There we were, busting our butts around this so-called athletic track. The Australian team coach was putting us through the rigors of a typical set of 25 × 400s in descending mode.

For years I made a living by leaving the field in my wake in the final discipline of my beloved sport of triathlon, but on this particular day there were two younger kids giving me a run for the money! First was 17-year-old Courtney Atkinson (who would go on to compete in two Olympics), and then there was Craig Alexander.

At this particular camp, selections for the upcoming world championship and world cup races were announced, and Craig wasn't selected for any of them! At that time I had approached the national team high-performance director to express my interest in putting forward our best legs, those being Craig's.

Why would I do such a thing? I don't know; maybe I believed I had an eye for talent. My intentions went terribly awry—the director told me that Craig wasn't even considered a B teamer but a C teamer!

"C'mon," I said (with quite a few expletives!), "if you can't see this talent, then you may as well run around with your blinkers on!"

In hindsight it may have been the best thing to happen to Craig, adding to the hunger of a caged tiger ready to go.

You may already know a little about Craig Alexander: He is a five-time world champion. Craig has won the sport's greatest prize, the Ironman® World

Championship, three times; he has won the Ironman 70.3® World Championship twice and counting. He has also won a monumental number of titles at the Olympic distance and 70.3 distance. Then there is his world record in Kona and the fact that he recently broke 8 hours in Melbourne and took home the Greg Welch trophy (shameless plug).

At age 39, Craig isn't finished yet. A battle with another over-39 athlete, Cameron Brown, in Melbourne drove Craig to his sub–8 hours. The next two years may possibly turn out to be Craig's finest!

Let's talk about Mark Allen for a minute: six Ironman crowns, ten Nice titles, and the sport's first Olympic-distance world champion. And Dave Scott has been a key influence for Craig with his six Ironman world crowns. These two were possibly the greatest ever . . . until Craig!

It's a familiar argument in the sport—who is the best or was the best—but to these guys it doesn't matter because they are humble champions, and that's not all that matters.

What else matters? In a word, family. Craig is the most loyal and trusting friend I think I have. We don't spend that much time together anymore, but I know exactly what he is like because I also strive each and every day for the same goal: to be the world's best dad and husband.

What professional athlete picks up his whole family and moves them around the world as regularly as Craig does?

He is so driven and he doesn't want his young children to miss a beat, to miss seeing Daddy win a race or to be a part of it themselves! To have the love of his life, Nerida, by his side sharing in the glory. It's Team Crowie, not his own glory, that keeps his clock ticking.

As you will discover in reading this book, it's no wonder Craig is one of the greatest triathletes ever. Words like "battle-hardened" say it all to me. He is ready for what's thrown at him, whether in training, racing, or life itself.

Craig's commitment to his sport is extraordinary, from the relentless pursuit of the perfect training day to recovery in Boulder Creek (where I first courted my wife after a 120-miler) to Neri filling the bath with ice awaiting Craig's return from training. Having a spouse like Neri who is always willing to take one for the team is an integral part of this puzzle.

As the Crow Flies is filled with riveting stories of commitment, setbacks, focus, and keeping it old school, probably what I like most. You see, these days most athletes have coaches and are pushing science more than feel. Craig is a feely type of guy and has proven that old school still works, and you have to agree . . . it works well!

Finally, the photography in this book is not only award winning but will act as a piece of art on any coffee table or bookshelf—this book simply has it all.

—GREG WELCH

FOUR-TIME WORLD CHAMPION

TOGETHER WITH THE FAMILY
at Cronulla Beach. The pro athlete
career is not a solo one; the family
is always a big part of it.

I was invited to join the Australian triathlon team for a training camp at Thredbo in the Snowy Mountains in January 1997. I was pretty new to triathlon, still finishing my studies at university. Following an easy training day, which was not a common occurrence at this camp, some of us gathered around the television to watch surf Iron Man racing, a popular sport in Australia. Jonathan Crowe flashed across the screen ("Crowie" made his name by winning the Coolangatta Gold, an iconic surf lifesaving race in Australia, in 1991. He was also a three-time winner in the Uncle Toby's Super Series and a winner of multiple Australian and world titles. He also appeared on the 1990s TV drama *Baywatch*).

One of the boys picked up on a striking resemblance between Crowie and me. I can't remember who was the culprit behind the nickname, but the guys there that day—Greg Welch, Chris Hill, Trent Chapman, Greg Bennett, Steve Croft, and Jason Harper—made sure the nickname stuck.

Introduction

Going into the 2011 season I was coming off my worst result in Kona, a fourth-place finish. It wasn't my worst performance. I was disappointed, but not disillusioned.

I was answering a lot of questions about my age and my perspective on where I was in my career. When you get to your late 30s in professional sport the questions about retirement are inevitable. It's the nature of the business, and people tend to try to make it easy for you by stating, "You don't have to prove anything," or "There is nothing left to achieve."

Personally, I always thought there was more for me to give both physically and mentally. But as is always the case, I turned to my best friend before making any big decisions about life or triathlon. My wife, Neri, intuitively knew I wanted to continue racing at the highest level, and she told me unequivocally that I had her full support. From that moment on I never thought about retirement again.

My entire career has depended on this kind of support from my family. I'm acutely aware of the demands placed on my family, and going into the 2011 season I needed to know that what I was doing wasn't negatively impacting them. That was enough for me.

Triathlon is generally considered an individual pursuit. If you ask anyone who races at any level, whether it be to win a world title or simply to finish a race and tick it off their bucket list, they will tell you that it's anything but individual. You need to be part of a great team. For me it all starts and finishes at home: Neri is the team captain. I've always received great emotional support from our extended families and friends.

What was left to achieve? The same as always: the pursuit of excellence in my performance. The never-ending desire to raise the bar.

I never once thought about being satisfied with what was already on the mantle. I am never one to look back in that sense, always forward.

COMMITMENT Early-season training

I made a commitment to myself from the very beginning to be the best athlete I could be.

When I first took up the sport of triathlon, my approach was a selfish one—it had to be. The sense of invincibility and enthusiasm that comes with being in your early 20s and new to something allowed me to be single-minded about my sport. It was 24/7, 365 days a year. I was in relentless pursuit of improvement. Whatever success I have had was born from this mind-set.

Early on, my obsession with all the little details validated in my own mind my decision to become a professional athlete. It was never about proving others wrong but about proving myself right and eliminating my own doubt. But motivation changes with time. Life experiences shift perspective. What started out as a selfish pursuit evolved into something completely different.

Becoming a parent changed the way I saw everything. It was refreshing. That selfish cocoon in which I had been existing was suddenly gone. When my daughter, Lucy, was born, there was a massive shift in my focus. People would say, "There is more pressure now with another mouth to feed." This was true; however, I couldn't get past the fact that I felt there was less pressure. At least one person wasn't going to judge me on my results. I told myself, "This life-and-death pursuit, this quest you've been on, is not quite life-and-death anymore; in fact, it never was." I now get my motivation from my wife, Nerida, and my children, Lucy and Austin.

My resolve to be the best athlete I can be remains the same, but my mind-set is guided by constant self-evaluation. Life is balanced between my family and my sport. I'm able to turn my focus and intensity on and off without sacrificing the outcome.

In 2010 I hit a career turning point: I went into Kona as the two-time defending champion and didn't win. It wasn't a bad performance, but sometimes getting beaten can be a catalyst for change.

If I'm brutally honest, the writing was on the wall in 2009—there were deficiencies in my training. It was determination and mental toughness that got me over the line. The fact that I won Kona that year masked those deficiencies. My race plan was a little one-dimensional as well. I got complacent because I felt it would still ultimately bring me success. It's natural to resist change when you have had success doing things a certain way. The eternal challenge is to make changes before the beating.

Heading into 2011, I wanted to revise my race schedule, begin a more focused strength and conditioning program, adopt a different mental attitude and strategy in the races, and reexamine my equipment choices.

I raced a lot of big races in 2010. As a world champion you receive a lot of invitations to race, and I accepted many of those invitations because I felt a responsibility to be visible and to be competitive. It was a lot of pressure mentally and physically to maintain the rage all season.

The changes to World Triathlon Corporation's qualification criteria requiring me to validate my Kona spot meant an early-season Ironman was also now in the cards. Having to do a second Ironman in a season further changed the game.

As a competitor you want to race all of the time, but once you've been lucky enough to win a championship or major race, everything changes. As far as everyone else is concerned, only major titles add to your résumé. In 2010 I had a very successful season, winning 7 out of 11 races, but I didn't win in Kona. For me, the entire season now revolves around these major races and their outcomes.

My days of racing 15 to 20 times a year are over.

TRAINING WEEK **STRENGTH & CONDITIONING (2–3×)**

STABILITY / Swiss ball exercises, push-ups, hip bridging exercises, and exercises to strengthen the pelvic stabilizers

STRENGTH / Cycling- and running-specific exercises such as front squats, back squats, lunges, hamstring curls, back extensions, power cleans / 3 × 8–12 repetitions per exercise, concentrating on proper technique with a range of motion that simulates cycling or running for the muscle group being worked

Part of my commitment to being the best entails leaving no stone unturned in my training.

My endurance has continued to improve throughout my 30s, but aging has brought about inevitable declines in strength and speed. I knew I had to change my training to remain competitive.

I'm privileged to have access to some of the great triathlon legends, people whom I have long admired. With the help of Dave Scott, I built a strength training program that I began immediately after Kona in 2010. I was training in the gym three times a week, something I hadn't done since the start of my career.

The strength training sessions were tough, but I noticed big improvements straightaway—that's exciting when you have been at something for over 15 years. At the highest level of any sport, you can toil for hours to get minuscule improvements.

Once you reach the elite level of competition, the steepest part of your improvement curve is well and truly behind you, and the focus turns to making minor advances.

My strength and conditioning program reinvigorated me mentally and physically for the year ahead. I could see the benefits translating specifically into my running and cycling. It was really paying off.

The time in the gym was also a lot of fun. It took me back to my university days. In the mid-1990s I was studying at the University of Sydney as well as working a part-time job. There was a good gym on campus, and I didn't have much time to train, so I found myself there three times a week. I wasn't doing a lot of volume in those days, but I was still competitive and always thought that my fitness was based on a good strength program.

As a triathlete, I was a late starter. In my teenaged years, I was always interested in sports and competed in school athletics, cross-country, and water polo. I was part of a swimming club,

but I never formally trained in any of the triathlon disciplines. I took up triathlon in my early 20s while at the University of Sydney.

Soccer was my first sporting love; I played for 13 years. While it entails a lot of running, soccer is as much about sprinting and agility as endurance. Looking back, I think it built a great foundation of fitness for me.

Greg Rogers was my first real coach in any of the three disciplines. I worked with Greg for over a decade (1994–2005) and learned about more than just swimming. He gave me my first insights into what it takes to become a world-class athlete—what it takes to be successful. He was as much a "mind" coach as he was a swim coach.

My regular regimen was 5 sessions per week, totaling 20 to 30 kilometers. There were a handful of times we did a "hell week"—10 sessions over 5 days, 5 kilometers per session. Now I swim three times a week with a local masters squad. There are a lot of high-caliber swimmers, including Surf Life Savers

(volunteer lifeguards), triathletes, and competitive open-water swimmers. I've always enjoyed training with single-discipline athletes. It's a good way to push yourself physically and mentally and concentrate on form and technique.

There are many advantages to training in a group setting. I find it easier to do the weekly volume. Each lane has five or six people who share the lead and the work. We are all on a similar cycle to build fitness and get faster, and the coach tailors the program to help each athlete achieve those goals.

I still value having a coach's eye above the water, someone who can see things that I don't feel. I might think I know where my head is or where my arms or hands are, but when I get tired my stroke can get a little rough. I welcome that edge-of-the-pool feedback because I always want to be learning and improving.

I also like to swim on my own for recovery at least once a week. It's nice not to be at the mercy of the clock or anyone else, and I can swim by feel. But there is no escaping the work.

TRAINING WEEK **SWIMMING**

MASTERS WORKOUT (3×) / 1–1½ hr. freestyle intensive / 2–3 km main set / Strength sets: pull buoy and paddle work mixed in year-round | **RECOVERY WORKOUT (1–2×)** / 1–1½ hr.

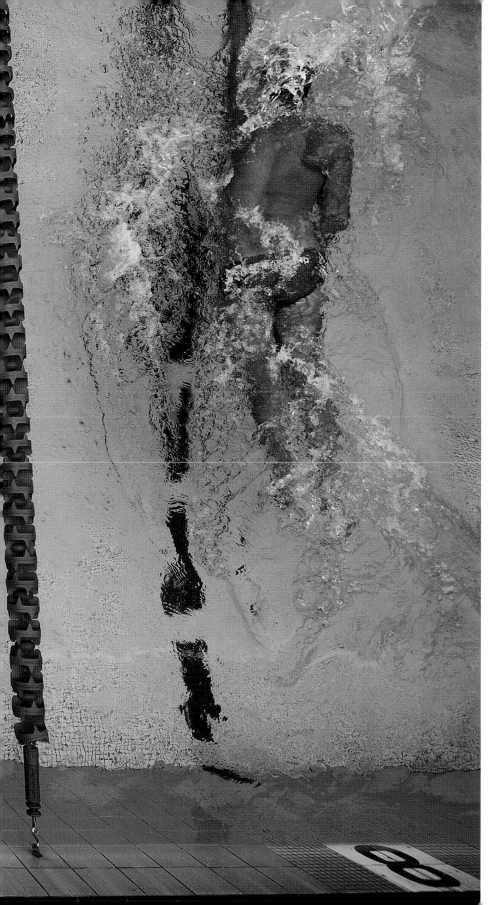

TEMPO WORKOUT

Warm-up / 500 (stroke count, concentrating on technique) / 500 mixed stroke/drill / 8 × 50 freestyle

Main set / Close to race pace, with short rest (usually 1:20/100 m) / 3 × 400 / 6 × 200 / 6 × 100 / As the summer progresses, recovery gets progressively shorter.

Cooldown / 200 stroke count

Total distance / 4.6 km

SPEED WORKOUT

Warm-up / 500 easy swimming (concentrating on technique) / 500 (50 right arm, 50 left arm, 100 choice drill, 100 backstroke, 100 freestyle, 50 right arm, 50 left arm) / 8 × 100 paddles, pull buoy, band (leaving on 1:20 or 1:30)

Main set / 8 × 400 / 1st 400 (150 easy, 50 hard × 2) / 2nd 400 (100 easy, 100 hard × 2) / 3rd 400 (50 easy, 150 hard × 2) / 4th 400 hard / Repeat sets. / Relatively short rest between each 400. Hard effort = faster than race pace.

Cooldown / 200 recovery

Total distance / 5.2 km

Note: Swim workouts are done in a long-course 50-meter pool. This basic framework can be used all year by tightening the intervals and shortening recovery.

I train in Australia from November to April, which is generally my preseason. It is always a priority to spend time with the kids as well as train.

It's important for me to get that balance.

Otherwise the training becomes all-consuming—which is what it needs to be to win, but it's hard to maintain that mind-set year-round.

I love my time with Lucy and Austin. I believe my job first and foremost is to be a good husband and father; triathlon comes third. We're an active family, and activity comes naturally to the kids. A lot of our time is spent in the pool, at the beach, or paddleboarding, basically just enjoying where we live.

I CAN'T RUN PAST Cronulla Beach without stopping to chat with local celebrity and lifeguard John Wilken. Legend has it Wilko raced the first triathlon ever held in Australia.

5 A.M. / CAPTAIN COOK BRIDGE, CRONULLA //

Early-morning starts are still tough.

I'm not a big fan of riding while it is still dark, but most of the other riders have day jobs, so we get it done early.

For the past 15 years, this has been a staple ride: It's the same route, same time every Tuesday and Thursday when I'm training in Australia.

We roll out at 5 a.m., riding against the peak-hour flow of traffic. It's safer that way. Ten years ago you wouldn't see a car for the first hour of this ride. It's a different story now, with a constant flow of traffic.

The group is normally made up of 15 to 20 people, and most of the riders are of a very high standard. It's a privilege to have so many good athletes to train with on a regular basis. The caliber of athletes really lifts the pace of the workout, particularly on my harder days.

TRAINING WEEK **CYCLING**

| **ENDURANCE RIDES (2×)** / Long aerobic endurance ride: 4–5½ hr., can incorporate hills | **TIME TRIAL SESSION** / 4–5 × 10 km efforts at race pace (sustainable threshold) within a 2–2½ hr. ride | **SPEED WORKOUTS (1–2×)** / 5 × 5 min. at race pace, 3 min. recoveries // **Or** 20 × 1 min. max efforts, 1 or 2 min. recoveries | **RECOVERY RIDES (1–2×)** / 1½–3 hr. at low intensity |

RIDE FROM CRONULLA TO WOLLONGONG //

It's not just about winning. It's about doing all of the little things, putting the processes in place for that positive outcome—a good race-day performance.

Indoor workouts are high-intensity speed or strength workouts during which I closely monitor power output.

These sessions are punishing, and by the time I'm finished there is a considerable puddle of sweat on the floor. This sort of intensity work is a necessary evil because it gets me race-ready. During one particular session, I did 20 1-minute efforts averaging 390 watts.

I have been using a power meter since I started competing in the Hawaii Ironman in 2007. Having a power meter on my bike is a good way to monitor my efforts and my fitness during specific workouts, but I also use it to ensure that I don't overtrain.

I am not really a number-crunching athlete. I don't use heart rate to monitor my training or fitness. When I started out as a university student, I couldn't afford a heart rate monitor, so I learned to do a lot of my sessions by feel (using rate of perceived exertion). In hindsight, I'm glad I learned this way because it has made me more attentive and attuned to my body's cues and my internal feedback. My degree in physiotherapy is helpful in this approach as well. I believe most racing is done by feel, not by a predetermined set of numbers or a formula.

STRENGTH WORKOUT

Warm-up / 10 min. easy spinning **/** 5 min. alternating 30 sec. max effort in a big gear, cadence of 70–80 rpm, with 30 sec. rest **/** 5 min. easy spinning

Main set options / 6 × 5 min. seated effort at cadence of 50–60 rpm, 2 min. easy spin recovery **// Or** 5 × 8 min. seated effort at cadence of 50–60 rpm, 2 min. easy spin recovery

Cooldown / 10 min. easy spin

SPEED WORKOUT

Warm-up / 10 min. easy spinning **/** 5 min. alternating 30 sec. max effort in a big gear, cadence of 70–80 rpm, with 30 sec. rest **/** 5 min. easy spinning

Main set options / 8 × 3 min. at race cadence of 85–90 rpm, 2 min. easy spin recovery **// Or** 20 × 1 min. at race cadence of 90–100 rpm, 1 min. easy spin recovery **/** Hardest effort sustainable for the predetermined interval.

Cooldown / 10 min. easy spin

Note: The goal is minimal variance between the first and last interval. Be mindful of this when determining effort in first interval and number of intervals.

THIS RUN begins in my hometown of Cronulla and goes to Boat Harbour and back.

I like to run alone. As with the other disciplines, every training session has a purpose.

It's important that I keep my focus in training so that I can hit the specific goals of each session. And again, as with the other disciplines, the idea is to develop the ability to maintain speed and technique even when you are starting to fatigue.

At the start of a run I'm specifically concentrating on my posture, leg turnover, and breathing. I used to remind myself to relax, especially when I was running fast. With experience and a lot more core strength, that process of relaxing became more subconscious.

In the preseason my strength runs are either hill repeats or running in the sand dunes near Cronulla Beach. Most of these kilometers are not superfast.

For a speed run, I'll do fast efforts at or slightly above race pace, with short recoveries. I enjoy playing with the speed. I usually try to get 20 to 30 minutes of quality work in during a speed-focused run. These workouts are affected by variables such as whether the session is done at altitude or sea level, what time of year it is, what my level of fitness is, and a subjective analysis of how I am feeling and coping with the demands of my overall program.

My long run can range anywhere from 1 hour 40 minutes to 2.5 hours and can include efforts as well. The length and intensity of my long run ramps up when I'm preparing for a race. Usually I do these runs the day after a race-simulation session or a brick session. Depending on what time of year it is, my run mileage will be somewhere between 60 and 120 kilometers per week.

TRAINING WEEK **RUNNING**

STRENGTH WORKOUT (2×) / Hill repeats / Running the dunes	**SPEED WORKOUT (2×)** / *Straight off the bike* / 6 × 3 min., 2 min. recovery **// Or** 6 × 5 min., 2 min. recovery	**LONG RUN (1–2×)** / 1 hr. 20 min.–2½ hr. either as a steady run, a negative split run, or longer intervals (greater than 5 min.) at goal race pace

I don't like the word "diet." To me, it implies some crazy regimen that you are constantly trying to stick to.

My wife is a great cook, and as a family we have what I consider a normal eating plan. We eat red meat, chicken, and fish a couple of times a week, as well as pasta once a week.

My training schedule is so strict that I don't like to waste time and mental energy worrying about food. It's easier for me to have a commonsense approach to nutrition. My main priority is to eat and drink enough to speed recovery so the next session can be as good as or better than the last.

During periods of heavy training I supplement my calorie intake with protein shakes. I also take zinc as well as a multivitamin to boost my immune system and branched-chain amino acids for recovery purposes. Electrolytes are also an everyday essential to aid in hydration.

In Australia I'm a little more flexible because it's preseason. I have learned over the years that it is important to relax at particular times to give myself a break, both mentally and physically. From July through September, I'm on high alert, vigilant with nutrition and supplements, letting my body know it's game time.

If I said my eating habits are textbook, I'd be lying because I eat a lot of chocolate, I love ice cream, I enjoy doughnuts, and I drink coffee. If I want to treat myself, I will. If I'm out with the kids and they are having an ice cream, I will have one too. If I feel like having a beer with dinner, I'll do that. Everything in moderation—but I'm disciplined enough not to do anything that will have a negative impact on my training the next day.

FOX SPORTS PROGAM *THE LONG LUNCH* / SYDNEY, AUSTRALIA //

I love the sport of triathlon, and I have been very fortunate to have had some success in it.

With that success comes the business side of sport.

Now I am not only an athlete but also a brand spokesperson and ambassador. Standing in front of a camera and appearing at speaking engagements have become the norm.

I don't fear them, but I'm certainly self-conscious, and I get nervous before each and every appearance. It doesn't hurt like racing or training, but it certainly takes me out of my comfort zone.

The serious part of my job remains to train and race. If the performances are good, fortunately, you don't need to do much talking.

FOCUS A new goal comes into view

The inaugural Ironman 70.3 World Championship in Florida in 2006 was the first world championship crown I won. By winning that title I automatically qualified for Kona, so my Kona career commenced the following year. The problem for me was that Ironman Hawaii, a full-Ironman-distance race, fell a month before the half-Ironman championship in Florida. As the reigning world champion at Ironman 70.3 I felt an obligation to go back and contest the race again in 2007, but the fatigue from finishing Ironman Hawaii just weeks prior made a consecutive Ironman 70.3 world championship a bridge too far. I had a good day, finishing in fourth place, but not the great day that you need to be crowned the champion. This ate away at me because even to this day, I believe the half-Ironman distance is my best distance.

In late 2010 the World Triathlon Corporation (WTC) announced a new date and location for the half-Ironman world title: It would now be contested in Las Vegas, four weeks before Kona. When this change was announced, I was pumped. Historically, throughout my Kona career, I had always felt that my best race of

the year was four weeks before the actual race in Kona. I was able to come down from altitude just two to three days prior to an event, maximizing that advantage, and heat acclimation wasn't as much of an issue for that first race. Now, without having to alter my schedule, I would get to race an Ironman 70.3 four weeks before Kona. And the real kicker . . . I would be racing for a world title. My season goal was set—I wanted to win the double.

I decided to validate my Kona slot in Port Macquarie on May 1. This race was a good fit with my schedule because I could get it done early in the season, and it gave me an opportunity to race at home, in front of my family and friends.

The Abu Dhabi International Triathlon, which fell seven weeks before Port Macquarie, seemed to fit perfectly into my early-season Ironman buildup. This event was particularly attractive thanks to its large prize purse, the chance to race in an exotic location, and plenty of media hype surrounding it.

IN THE LAST WEEK before a long, hot race, I'm not doing a lot of training. For Abu Dhabi I did two to three light one-hour sessions each day. You need to keep the body moving, but you don't want to go overboard. It's more important to try to stay out of the heat before the race.

I'VE BEEN DOING THIS A LONG TIME. I'm usually relaxed right before a race, but I knew it would be a long day in Abu Dhabi. In longer races I can become more nervous because I know it's going to hurt and it's going to be tough. There's always a fear of the unknown. It's human nature to be anxious when you've worked hard and hope for a good result.

ABU DHABI INTERNATIONAL TRIATHLON
ABU DHABI, UNITED ARAB EMIRATES // MARCH 12, 2011 //
3K swim / 200K bike / 20K run

6:59 A.M. / 1.5 KILOMETERS //

100 KILOMETERS //

It was an extremely windy race, and the temperature climbed to 37°C (98°F). I cramped up severely during the last hour of the bike.

This usually happens for one of two reasons: extreme fatigue or salt depletion. I hung with the leaders for as long as I could, and that took its toll on me later. The cramping continued through the entire run. My legs were as stiff as boards, and I had to sprint to finish in sixth place.

The level of fitness I had at that point in the season wasn't quite enough for me to be in the lead. Sometimes your level of fitness just doesn't match your desire. I raced to my potential and was simply beaten by other guys who had better days than I did. It was a hard race, and it hurt me a lot.

I got the most out of myself, so the numbers didn't matter. I felt that Abu Dhabi had increased my fitness by 2 or 3 percent. I accomplished my objective, and I was feeling good. Looking forward, my intention was to return home, recover, and then knuckle down to start my serious push into Port.

There's also a social component to racing. I have known and raced against a lot of my competitors for a decade or more. Over the years some have become good friends.

Often we are training in different corners of the globe and the only time we catch up is at the races. In Abu Dhabi, I spent some time with Paul Matthews while taking a post-race ice bath at the hotel. "Barney," who grew up in northern New South Wales, trains with me when we are both in Boulder and hangs out with us.

I have media and sponsorship commitments around most races.

In Abu Dhabi I was asked to speak to students at the American International School. When talking to young people, I typically discuss the ins and outs of being a professional athlete, the demands as well as the rewards. I also address the difficulty I had early on with balancing education and training, and later on with balancing family and sponsorship with training.

Students typically ask how much money I make, who my sponsors are, and do they give me free stuff. I try to tell them that being a professional athlete is not a guarantee. I made sure I got the best marks I could and went on to graduate as a physiotherapist. I try to explain that, for me, being a professional athlete has never been about the money. I do it because I love it. I enjoy being able to interact with students and answer questions about the sport.

Abu Dhabi was the first time in my career that I had the opportunity to race on a purpose-built Formula 1 track. A section of the track was included in the racecourse, and the following day the track was the site for Shimano's 2012 product catalog photo shoot. This time around, the ride was a bit more leisurely. Along with the other sponsored athletes, I had a great time swinging in and out of the corners, taking off from the pits, working next to the race strips, and riding along the starting grid.

WHEN I RETURN from longer trips, Neri and the kids do a formal pickup. Lucy loves making me a "Welcome Home" sign. It means a lot—I race for my family, so these moments are special.

WE WENT TO WATCH some of our friends race at the ITU World Championship series race in Sydney.

IN THE PRE-RACE press conference just days before Ironman Port Macquarie, I announced that I would be pulling out of the race due to illness.

SETBACKS Holding it together when things fall apart

The Abu Dhabi International Triathlon in March was the only race I competed in before I got sick. It was seven weeks out from Ironman Port Macquarie, and I came home after the race to an easy recovery week before beginning my heavy training for Port Macquarie.

A rough night of light fevers and little sleep was supposed to be followed by a long early-morning ride. During the night I thought, "If I wake before the alarm goes off I will get up and go for the ride. But if the alarm wakes me or if it's hard to get up, I'll take the day off—my body will need it."

I woke up before the alarm, so I rode, but it was a tough day. Actually, it was awful. I was weak and something was clearly wrong. It was the start of a severe respiratory virus and, by extension, the start of a problematic few months.

I was aiming to win Port, and it was my validating race for Kona, so when it became obvious that I wouldn't be healthy enough to compete, I was disappointed. I went along to fulfill sponsorship and media obligations, but at the time I was deep in the throes of the virus, constantly coughing and occasionally needing sleeping pills just to get some rest.

Missing Port Macquarie really put a spanner into the works in terms of my Kona validation. I still needed to fit in another Ironman, and now I knew it wasn't going to happen in the early stages of the season, as I had hoped.

In the midst of my sickness, I never stopped to reassess my goal: I still intended to put in benchmark performances at Vegas and Kona. The lead-up was just going to look and feel different. My schedule would have to change, but the goal never changed.

GREG WELCH
HAWAIIAN IRONMAN
TRIATHLON CHAMPION

SAUCONY

My career hasn't been riddled with illnesses and setbacks. In fact, it had been a good six years since I had last been seriously ill, with a liver virus.

I have never seen a doctor with any regularity—in fact, I didn't even have a regular doctor when this virus stopped me in my tracks. I knew I had to find medical practitioners who understood the physical demands I put on my body as well as the inherent problems with certain treatment protocols associated with being a professional athlete.

It was all there in my test results. My doctors were calling it "the hundred-day cough," and there was a lot of it going around Sydney.

There was no infection in my lungs, but something had attacked my upper airways and was causing them to narrow, as in asthma. I was coughing all day long; my airways would spasm and narrow, and I would cough to try to splint them open. I was having weekly checkups and being advised to take off weeks at a time. The diagnosis proved to be right; the cough was with me for four months.

Over the years I've occasionally had to navigate through these sorts of setbacks, and I've realized that things usually aren't as bad as they seem in the moment. In this case, I realized I would not be able to train anywhere near my full capacity for a couple of months. During that time I would have to be vigilant, make sure my eating habits were healthy, take good advice from the doctors, and plan things well in advance. I had deposited four great months of training in the fitness bank before I got sick. I knew I would be able to make a couple of big withdrawals later in the year. I just needed to be patient. It was frustrating, though. I was just so sick and tired of coughing.

MUCH OF NERI'S FAMILY lives near Port Macquarie, so Austin and Lucy were able to celebrate their birthdays (which are just a week apart) with some of their cousins. It was really the first time that either of our kids had celebrated a birthday with our extended family. Because I didn't have to race, we were also able to support Neri's sister Jules, who was racing her first half-Ironman.

ONCE WE RETURNED TO CRONULLA, Neri put together a cupcake-decorating party for Lucy and her friends. The house was full of little girls in matching aprons having a blast.

I've been going to the United States to train and race since 2002. Neri has always traveled with me.

When Lucy was born in 2005, Neri and I made a pact to always travel as a family. This brought some financial pressure, but timing is everything. When Lucy was just eight weeks old, I won the Lifetime Fitness Triathlon in Minnesota, which was the largest prize purse in the sport of triathlon at the time. Winning that race freed us up so that Neri could take time off every year from her work as an emergency nurse and travel with me.

We now split our time between Australia and the United States. Boulder, Colorado, has become our U.S. base for up to four months of the year. We've got a good system worked out now, but it's still punishing to pack up the family for that length of time.

We arrive at the airport with a mountain of luggage—it's a nightmare. Just keeping the kids corralled long enough to get through check-in is a challenge. When the aircraft doors finally close Neri and I both breathe a huge sigh of relief, though I don't know if the people sitting in our row can say the same.

On one of these flights, Aussie was running the dimly lit aisles when everyone was meant to be sleeping. With the curiosity of a two-year-old, he lifted a lady's eye mask to see if she was really sleeping, and then he tried to pull her socks off. Needless to say, she wasn't amused, and she let Neri and me know it in no uncertain terms.

Traveling with family is hard given the long flights, connections, security lines, and time-zone changes. But it is just a means to an end, and my career has afforded us all a great lifestyle.

We have a complete life in Australia and a complete life in the United States as well, so the kids don't miss out on anything. It's always full-on wherever we are. When they are in the United States, they don't pine for home—but likewise, when we are home, they don't pine for Boulder either. Wherever Mum and Dad are is where they love to be. That's home.

Escape from Alcatraz was my first race in 2011 in the United States.

I had committed to the race earlier in the year, and I felt a big obligation to uphold my commitment.

Race organizers and sponsors are generally understanding in these situations, but at the time, I just wanted to get back into racing.

I knew I wasn't in great shape. The doctor I was seeing, Martin Jaffe, laid it out for me: "You are not 100 percent healthy, but you are going to have to do your first race sooner or later." I figured I may as well do it

sooner and blow out the cobwebs. It would be a litmus test to see where I was physically.

It's hard going into a race with that mind-set, knowing your health and fitness are not at 100 percent. I had completely missed three weeks and just begun to ease back into training. At this point my main concern was validating my Kona spot, which I planned to do at Coeur d'Alene in three weeks. I wanted to put a positive spin on it, so at the very least this race was going to be like a very hard

training day, which I felt would help with my fitness moving forward. In hindsight, it was a mistake to race.

We arrived Friday; the race was Sunday. I had been sick for so long that my chest was constantly aching from the incessant coughing. After lifting my bike case at the airport, I felt a quick, sharp pain in my ribs. It faded away. As a professional athlete, you make a point of removing all negativity from your thoughts. You become accustomed to shunning excuses, but in this instance I should have seen the red flag.

knuckles
at the wharf

5:20 A.M., JUNE 5 / SAN FRANCISCO //

The starting cannon fired, and I jumped off the deck of the *San Francisco Belle* into the icy waters off Alcatraz Island.

When I hit the 12°C (57°F) water, there was a big reflex inhalation. I felt that sharp pain again. It was an uphill battle from there. I could hardly get my right arm out of the water to swim, and I was already well behind the leaders. It was a different kind of pain than what I am used to feeling in a race, and I knew something was definitely wrong. I made up some time on the bike because the cold air numbed the pain. The run, on the other hand, was very painful. I steadily dropped back through the field. I had it in my mind to finish, and I did, but it was one of the toughest races of my career.

7:54 A.M.

9:02 A.M.

9:31 A.M.

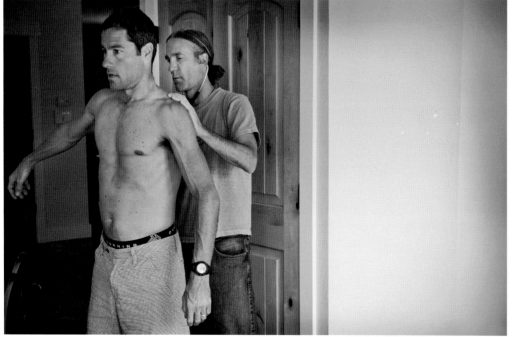

THE MOST IMPORTANT THING in the weeks following Alcatraz was to manage the pain. I didn't need a definitive diagnosis. As a qualified physiotherapist, I had a fair idea of what was going on, so I consciously put off having an MRI. I had it in my mind that I was going to validate at Coeur d'Alene in three weeks and nothing was going to derail that thought process.

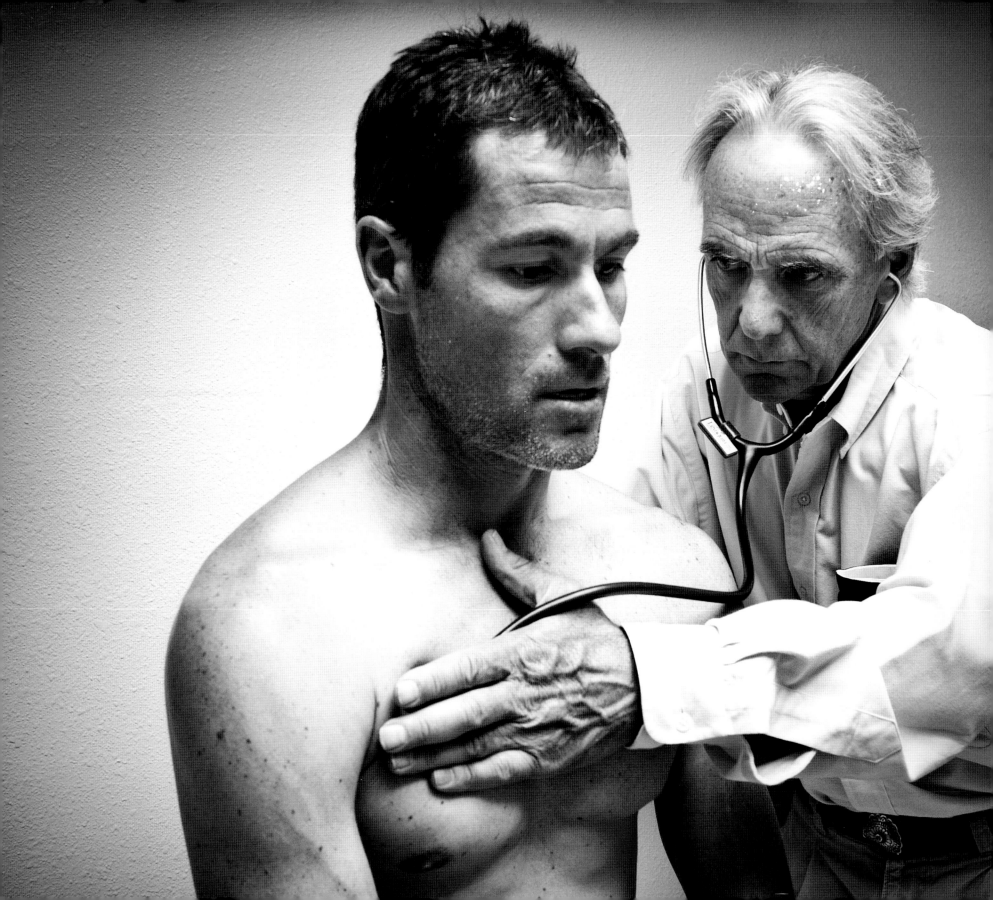

I was already in the middle of a troubled season when a partnership on the business front was reaching boiling point.

As in any business, relationships can go sour. I needed to resolve the situation, which wouldn't be pleasant or easy. I knew it could get messy, and I knew there would be fallout publicly and privately.

In looking at the bigger picture, I had to consider the eighteen other sponsors who had invested time and money in me. I knew it wasn't fair to the rest of the team to be so mentally distracted with business issues. I wasn't going to let this disruption compromise my ability to be a great brand ambassador for my other sponsors. This was uncharted territory after a decade and a half in the sport and many long-term partnerships.

After much thought and discussion, it became clear to me that there was only one option and that was to negotiate an end to my Orbea sponsorship. I grieved initially over ending the relationship; seven years is a long time to work with a sponsor, and making a change after such a long and successful partnership is difficult. But I knew I had to move on. I felt it wasn't the right fit anymore; we had both capitalized on the relationship. It was time to pursue new opportunities and new directions.

It would take months for my decision to play out in public. And the timing was dreadful; I still needed to qualify for Kona at Ironman Coeur d'Alene when this erupted. It was a stressful two weeks leading up to that race— I was still sick, I was racing on minimal training, and I now had this sponsorship drama going on.

Irrespective of the challenges I faced going into Coeur d'Alene, on race day it felt great to compete.

I was able to put everything out of my mind and just race. No talk, no e-mails. I was alone and doing what came naturally. I left it on the track. I won Coeur d'Alene, broke the course record, and validated for Kona.

That was the moment when the earlier block of training in the year came to fruition. As I had hoped, the four months of training was all there. I was fitter than I thought. I started to see a lot of positive momentum. I made it through this eight-hour race fairly unscathed, not having to fire on all cylinders, so the post-race recovery was going to be good. The rib was well on the way to healing, and the cough was starting to subside. The race was like therapy. I could now put a lot of this behind me and just focus on the dream: Las Vegas and Kona.

The MRI I got after Coeur d'Alene confirmed that my 11th rib was fractured as a result of months of coughing. Add to that my mistake of doing

Alcatraz—a short, high-intensity race in such conditions with a respiratory virus. In hindsight it would have been smarter to start off with a middle-distance race in a warmer climate, although with a broken rib it may not have mattered.

As a professional athlete, I've learned to control what I can and try not to be overly concerned with the rest. That four months of training was all still there. If I had been sick in January, my season preparation would have been severely limited, but my preseason was actually very good. I was on my way to getting healthy.

Looking back, I think perhaps my poor performance at Alcatraz had a silver lining. It got me off the radar and removed much of the pressure I typically feel at this point of the season, with constant interviews around Kona and contenders. With everybody off my back, I was free to focus on my recovery.

IRONMAN COEUR D'ALENE / IDAHO / JUNE 26, 2011 //
2.4 mile swim / 112 mile bike / 26.2 mile run

A successful athletic career can get very busy and overwhelming if you let it.

I'm not a control freak—I don't need to oversee every aspect of my career. I am happy to delegate to people I trust, and I consider myself very lucky to have assembled such an exceptional team. If there is one thing I have been able to do consistently well, it is scouting great talent that can add value both to me personally and to my career.

I have amazing mechanics, sponsors, mentors, coaches, massage therapists, and training partners as well as great products to work with. A lot of people go above and beyond for me: They stay up all night building my bikes and preparing my equipment; they provide support and years of wisdom. These are the people I have the privilege to work with and to learn from. It often goes beyond business, and my family and I consider many of these people to be true friends.

At the end of the day all I really want to do is train and be a good husband and father. It's my job to be in great shape, and fortunately that's what I get to concentrate on most of the time. When you can keep it simple like that and you know you've got great people around you, it completely minimizes the stress associated with racing at a high level.

On a long raining ride up in the mountains in 2009, Tim DeBoom told me about this great mechanic in North Boulder. Tim couldn't remember his name, so on returning from the ride I did an online search and found Chuck Panaccione at Superfly Cycles. I called him cold. His wife, Celeste, suggested that I come around the next day. At the time Chuck was working out of his garage for a company called Enduro Bearings, installing ceramic bearings. I engaged Chuck to do some work for me. It was September, about a week or two before we were leaving for Kona.

When I went around to pay for the work, Chuck, knowing I was the reigning Ironman world champion, offered to do the work for nothing and suggested a sponsorship relationship. I felt strongly about paying for the work that he had done, but I asked him to meet up with my manager at Interbike. After I won in Kona, we formalized the relationship, and I've been working with Chuck ever since.

In a similar fashion, my relationship with Newton was born.

In 2007, I was running in Nike shoes. While I didn't have a formal sponsorship with Nike, I was getting free shoes from a local sales rep in Sydney. My friend John Duke suggested in April 2007 that I make contact with Danny Abshire when I got to Boulder later that year and try the Newton shoes. Newton was a brand-new running-shoe company in its start-up year. After a bit more prodding from John, I went to meet Danny for the first time, and we hit it off immediately. A podiatrist and avid runner, Danny was the inventor of the forefoot technology incorporated in the Newton shoes. His thoughts on running form and training really resonated with me.

After assessing my technique in the Newton car park, Danny gave me a pair of shoes. He told me to break them in slowly, but after that first run in the car park I could tell they were a perfect fit for me and I did a two-hour-long run the very next day.

I was about to start the serious buildup for my first assault on the Hawaii Ironman. I decided to entrust my preparation to Newton running shoes. I had no formal arrangement—I received great advice from Danny, and Newton gave me shoes as needed. I contacted the Nike sales rep back in Sydney to say I had found something better and would like to move on. I was pretty sure a massive company like Nike wasn't going to miss a little triathlete like me, and I was right. I instinctively felt that there would be performance benefits to running in this shoe.

The rest is history. Four months later I finished second in my Kona debut, and my official sponsorship relationship with Newton started shortly thereafter.

Sometimes the best relationships are born out of your own curiosity and desire to seek out the people and equipment that are going to add value to your performance. It's not always about money. The money comes later if you perform well.

GOING SOLO Building up to the world championships

I've been coming to Boulder since 2005. It's a beautiful place to train. It offers great training variety, good people to train with, extensive facilities, and a family atmosphere. Neri and the kids love living there. We have found a community of athletes, some with children, and have enjoyed the social aspects as well. Boulder has a similar feel to Australia with its laid-back lifestyle and attitude . . . our home away from home.

My training is different and harder than in Sydney. It's the business end of the season—this is when it's time to really go to work. The days are completely based upon my training schedule, even for the family. It's a full-time job for all of us. I want to be at my best for the world championships.

Three months of an unrelenting Boulder training schedule helps me become mentally tougher, battle-hardened. As an athlete, you know when you've done the work required and more. You score those points in your head. That's the essence of my mental preparation. There is always a different feel when I leave Boulder because I know how I've trained and prepared. It's almost as if with my Boulder preparation, I've achieved my gold standard.

Boulder gives me great access to altitude training. But I've found that over time the benefits it offers to my fitness can reach a plateau because I am subjecting myself to the same stimuli year after year. So with every year I consistently train a little higher. Twice a week I run on Magnolia Drive, which starts at 2,438 meters (8,000 feet) above sea level and rises to about 2,896 meters (9,500 feet). I also run on what is known as the Switzerland Trail. These are famous running trails, and I often see some of the world's elite marathoners training.

When you're away from home, you work with what you've got.

It's impossible, both logistically and financially, to re-create everything that you've built at home elsewhere. It's great to have access to all of Boulder's facilities, but I didn't start my career with all of the bells and whistles, and I've learned to do without them. The truth is, I don't mind an old-school training environment; in fact, I thrive on it. I walk into our rented garage, and I know it's time to go to work.

All I need is my '80s music mix, my power meter, and plenty of fluids because it's hot as hell. If it's good enough for Rocky Balboa, it's good enough for me.

LATE SEASON TRAINING WEEK

SUNDAY	MONDAY	TUESDAY	WEDNESDAY
Long run 2–2½ hr. / Recovery swim / Tempo run (optional)	Gym / Swim 4 km / Ride 3 hr., hills / Run 30 min. easy	Tempo run 1 hr.–1 hr. 10 min. / Swim 4 km / Ride 1½–2 hr. easy	Long ride 4½–6 hr. / Run 30–40 min. off the bike, can be at goal marathon pace

THURSDAY
Ride 2 hr., with strength or speed efforts / Swim 4–5 km / Run 1 hr. 10 min.–1 hr. 40 min.

FRIDAY
Gym / Swim 4 km / Ride 2–3 hr. (optional) / Run 40 min. easy

SATURDAY
Ride 4 hr. / Run 1 hr. off the bike, with race-pace efforts

This is the framework I've used in the past for the final push phase of the buildup to an important race. With the optional workouts, this is the most training I would do in a single week.

THE ROCKY MOUNTAINS are full of hidden gems. Ward is a little town about 30 kilometers (19 miles) outside Boulder. It sits 2,880 meters (9,450 feet) above sea level along a popular cycling route. Everybody stops at this shop to get cookies, Coke, or whatever else they need for energy on their ride. A Boulder cycling enthusiast sponsors the water fountain.

When training at altitude my body doesn't recover the same way it does at sea level.

I have found that the same reason that athletes seek out high-altitude training, a lack of oxygen forcing the body to learn to adapt, slows my recovery. Because of this I've had to invoke extra techniques to assist my body in recovery.

I use NormaTec compression boots two or three times a day when I'm in Boulder for about half an hour at a time to improve my circulation. I notice the benefits immediately—the boots make my legs feel lighter, flushing out the heavy feeling that follows a long training session.

I also jump into an ice bath daily. This is something I usually do straight after heavy training sessions. Neri knows my training schedule and always has the ice bath ready. She and the kids ride

their bikes from our apartment to the convenience store to pick up bags of ice. The water is cooled to roughly 10°C (50°F). Sometimes I wade into Boulder Creek for a natural alternative to my regular ice baths. The kids will often come with me; they love to play by the creek.

Ten minutes in the ice bath prompts a physiological response, preventing the body from doing any more muscle damage. The cold numbs the pain and enhances circulation to flush out all of the by-products of hard exercise

and stimulate the nervous system. It's not enjoyable, but I feel 100 percent better afterward.

In Boulder there is more of a focus on these little details. I don't do all of these things year-round partly because when you take these extra measures, you know subconsciously that there is a race around the corner. You are cognitive of every little aspect. There's a feeling that the cards will fall where they may because you've done all you can.

The training scene in America differs quite substantially from that in Australia.

In Australia you train at different locations depending on what facilities you need. This is in direct contrast to the United States, where there is a large athletic club or gym culture. The Flatiron Athletic Club (FAC) is a big part of my training when we're in Boulder. It houses a range of facilities including pools, gyms, and tennis courts along with some world-class coaches. Dave and Jane Scott, Simon Lessing, and Wolfgang Dittrich all coach swimming at FAC, and most of the professional athletes in town train here. You can find our whole family here most days.

I'VE FOUND the profile of this stretch of road resembles the Queen K Highway in Kona, so it's a good race simulation session. The road also has mile markers, so I can monitor my pace closely if needed.

It was turning out to be the perfect summer.

Neri and the kids were having a great time with a lot of mini-golf, go-karts, eating out, and socializing. We were in a groove as a family, and I felt physically strong.

From a professional standpoint, my training sessions could not have been better. Some of them were even above and beyond, Hall of Fame sessions—ones you remember as benchmarks. I could feel the form coming.

A couple of weeks before the Ironman 70.3 World Championship in Las Vegas, I scouted the course with training partners Julie Dibens and Fraser Cartmell. That trip gave me more good feedback, and I knew I would be comfortable racing on this course. It was going to be windy, superhot, and hilly, and once again the synergy was there because I felt that my push phase was tailored to a strong performance at both of the

world championship races. I wasn't doing one at the expense of the other or using one as a stepping-stone. Despite that confidence, there was an undercurrent of skepticism suggesting that it was perhaps detrimental to attempt both races. I blocked it out—my plan seemed to be coming together perfectly.

When you put in the work in a sport like triathlon, it forms the cornerstone of your confidence. In the buildup, I didn't miss a session.

By the time I arrived in Las Vegas, I had finally stopped coughing. I was in great shape, and with every week the foundation was getting stronger. I was doing a large volume of work at a very good intensity. The momentum was building; I had dealt with the interruptions, and now it was time to play.

I came out of the water in the top 10. By kilometer 16 (mile 10) of the bike, I had assumed the lead. There was a front group of about eight guys, and I was at the head of the group when I got a flat tire. Luckily there was a tech support van on the course, and I was able to switch out the wheel quickly. Time stands still in these situations, and I felt as if I had lost about 30 seconds to 1 minute. It doesn't sound like much, but when your competitors are going at 45 kilometers (28 miles) per hour, even 30 seconds is significant.

I managed to catch the leaders by the turnaround at 40 kilometers (25 miles). I finished the bike segment in a tie for second place. It was a great position to be in, just 3 minutes down on supercyclist Chris Lieto. Chris and I have had some epic duels. I had to run him down to win my second title in Kona, and if I wanted to win another world title, I would have to do it again today. I took the lead about halfway into the run and eventually won by just over 3 minutes.

This win brought on a lot of emotion. After battling through what had felt like roadblocks all year, it was a massive relief to finally be at 100 percent and to win such a big race. I have always felt that I am best suited to the half-Ironman distance. Now I have two world titles at this distance: Clearwater, Florida, 2006 on a flat, fast course and Vegas 2011 on a hilly, windy course.

I bought a bike in Boulder three weeks before Vegas. After painstakingly considering every possible scenario, I was sticking to my convictions and riding a new bike for the first time publicly in Las Vegas. It's risky to make equipment changes so close to a major race; I'd been riding my sponsored bike for nearly seven years and experienced great success during that time. Moreover, from a legal standpoint, I couldn't be seen to be actively promoting another brand, so in my hotel on the day before the race I taped over the logo of the new bike.

6:53 A.M.

IRONMAN WORLD CHAMPIONSHIP 70.3 / LAS VEGAS, NV / SEPTEMBER 11, 2011 // 1.2 mile swim / 56 mile bike / 13.1 mile run

8:33 A.M. / 40 MILES //

9:59 A.M. / 9 MILES //

IN THE LEAD GROUP coming out of Lake Mead National Park, I crest the hill to see Dwight Woodforth, my good friend and training partner from Sydney (above). I've just finished the second run lap of three. Cheering me on are Neri, her younger sister Rachel (who made the trip from Australia to watch both Jules and me race), and Holly Bennett, a friend from Boulder (left).

10:23 A.M.

CROSSING THE LINE for world title number 4 (left). Embracing Neri at the finish (right).

WINNING THE WORLD CHAMPIONSHIP
in Las Vegas confirmed that my recovery from
the virus was finally complete and I could turn
in a great performance at a big race.

DRINK STOP AT ESTES PARK: On a regular ride, our group this particular day included (left to right) Dwight Woodforth, Tim Berkel, Mirinda Carfrae, Matt White, Chris Legh, me, and Tyler Butterfield (right). Peak to Peak Highway with Dwight Woodforth on a long training ride. Longs Peak can be seen in the background (below). Passing St. Malo church on the Peak to Peak Highway (opposite).

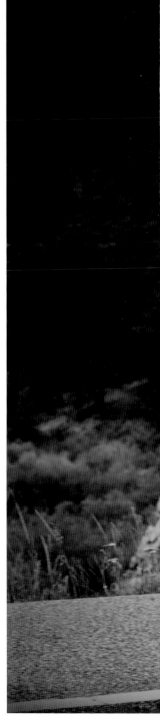

MY TECHNIQUE started to unravel a little on the way home. My hips were dropping. I was 10 minutes from home and ready to collapse into the ice bath.

Before we had kids, Neri would often accompany me on training sessions.

Neri's sister Jules made the trip with us to Boulder in 2011, which allowed Neri to join me on her mountain bike on some of my runs. Training with support always enables me to attain an extra level.

In one of my typical big brick sessions, I rode about six hours and went straight into a long run with three longer sustained efforts and then a run home. It was a seven-hour training day, similar in duration to the race. In a session like this, it's important to have nutrition and pacing support. When Neri rides alongside me, she supplies the electrolyte drinks and fuel that I would be able to get from an aid station on race day. I like to simulate the race so I can become efficient at using whatever fuel is available. It's also a great pacing exercise. I try to progressively push the intensity of each effort.

On this particular Saturday, we were focusing on maintaining speed. The first effort was at 2:36 marathon pace, and the last effort was at 2:24 marathon pace. It was much quicker than my actual race pace, but that's what I like to do in training: play with the speed. There is a mental lift from having someone else there; this session would have been brutal on my own.

It's necessary to occasionally subject your body to what it's going to get on race day. Obviously you can't do that every week. Building that endurance, overlaying and not breaking down, is the premise of endurance training. You overload, recover, overload, and hopefully each time you bounce to a slightly higher level and build up to a peak.

FINAL COUNTDOWN Returning to Kona

The Ironman World Championship is a tough event, promising the most challenging conditions and the best competition. Everyone on the start line has earned his or her spot. They are all exceptionally talented, and they have worked extremely hard. Every year there are 5 to 10 guys with a legitimate shot at winning Kona. I assume that all of my competitors will be at the top of their game. I've raced against most of them for the past 10 years or more. The media is quick to hype a rivalry or pick out an up-and-coming challenger, but come race day it could be someone you never expected who is having a great day.

I don't sit around obsessing about my competition. I do pay attention to race results, and I just assume that they are going to do exactly what I'm going to do, which is turn up at the biggest race in my best shape that I've exhibited this year, plus x percent. I know that if I race at my best, I'm going to be a handful.

There were several differences in my preparation for Kona this time around. In all four of my previous Kona campaigns, we had arrived at the big island nearly four weeks before the race. In 2011 I decided to go Kona just two weeks

before the race. It was a big change. It's a delicate balance to work out—the trade-off between the benefits of altitude and leaving yourself enough time to acclimate to Hawaii's heat.

I didn't overanalyze or overthink the decision. This time around I just felt ready. I felt bulletproof. My form was good, and so much hard work had gone into the preparation. I remained focused and paid attention to the little details. The work was done; it was time for a little polish.

Everyone at every level makes mistakes. You can do all the work but panic at the last minute and do something you shouldn't—something silly, something born out of insecurity or anxiety. Sometimes it can be difficult to back off when you feel like you should be doing more; it's the mentality of an athlete. It's happened to me.

In 2009, when I won Kona for the second time, I was coming off a terrific season. I felt pressure to replicate everything to the letter from the previous year,

where I had had a great performance. As a result, I made some bad decisions and pushed myself too hard in the buildup, not just with the training but in every aspect of the preparation.

Specifically, in the last month I didn't allow enough time for packing up our home in Boulder, traveling, and adequate recovery. I pulled a few consecutive all-nighters after racing Ironman 70.3 in Muskoka, Ontario. It caught up with me by the time we arrived in Hawaii. I got heat stress on my first day of training and passed out.

In spite of that I managed to win a second world championship, but it was more born out of mental toughness than a clinical physical performance. I was driven to put up a worthy title defense. I feel I was very lucky to win it.

Heading into Kona this time around, I fought the feeling that I should be doing more. I learned from my past mistakes and showed more maturity as an athlete.

I'm typically not one to dwell on past performances, particularly good ones. Once they are in the books, so to speak, my focus immediately turns to the next challenge. Following my victory at the Ironman 70.3 World Championship in Las Vegas, just four weeks out from Kona, I was able to exhale and enjoy it. I had won another world title. It didn't bring any extra burden or expectation.

Once we arrived in Hawaii the final lead-up wasn't without its nervous moments. But this time around there was a different feeling in the air. The kids were playful, and our family enjoyed many candid moments in the days before the race.

I don't believe in destiny in sport as such; you tend to get what you deserve. You can't control everything. You want to be able to capitalize on the good luck and overcome the bad luck. All the clichés ring true—you reap what you sow. Over the course of a career I think it all evens out.

Win or lose, in the end it falls on you as an athlete and a person. You can't hide behind excuses or accomplishments when you're out there racing. I didn't go into Kona believing that I would win or that I deserved to win; I just thought we had done everything we could.

FINALIZING my new sponsorship agreements with Specialized and TYR in the days leading up to the race.

BETWEEN the media and sponsorship appearances, race week brings with it a lot of obligations. I try to keep these to a minimum in order to avoid the whole thing turning into a circus. This time around it was especially important because there were more loose ends than usual (left).

CHRIS McCORMACK, the 2010 Kona winner, formally introduced me as a new member of the Specialized team at one of the pre-race events. When I look at this photo I laugh because I look like a cardboard cut-out in these shorts, fresh out of the packet. My sponsors send me all of their latest gear to wear during race week (above).

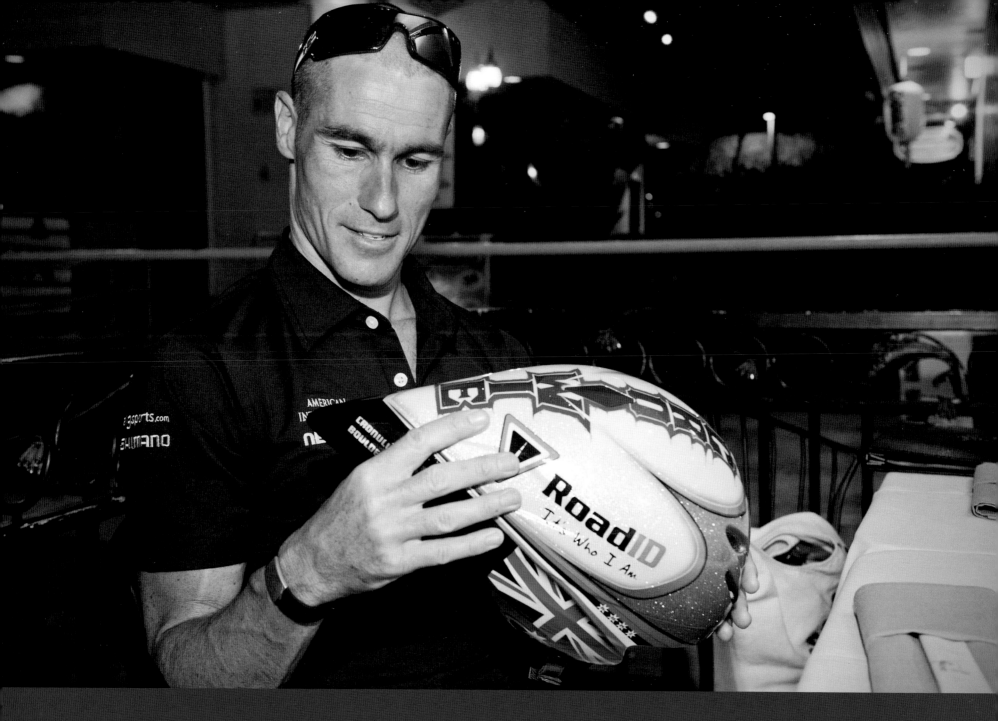

A few nights before the race Ed Wimmer and P.J. Rabice from Road ID surprised me with a custom helmet for race day. The personal detail in the artwork was amazing—the boys had really done their homework. The Australian flag was prominently featured, along with a star for each of my four world titles. My favorite detail was the names of Neri, Lucy, and Austin painted on the right side of the helmet. This would be the first year I used a time trial helmet in the race.

ONE OF THE FEATURES of my new bike was an integrated hydration system, which is functional and also has aerodynamic benefits.

I had only been riding my new Shiv for two and a half weeks before the race.

Switching bikes so close to any race is far from the ideal situation. But after speaking with Mark Cote from Specialized and having Mat Steinmetz painstakingly set the bike up, I rolled out of my garage and it felt like the bike was part of me. My first ride was an unbelievable motorpace session. My decision to ride the Shiv in Kona ultimately was a combination of factors: my ability to get a great position and the performance aspects of the bike itself. Forgetting all of the numbers, it just felt right.

When you have success as an athlete, you soon find that there are people around to consult with you on equipment and provide great technical support, but I still take it upon myself to make sure that my bike is riding perfectly. I consider it to be my responsibility.

IT SEEMS TO HAPPEN with uncanny regularity that Mark and I cross paths in race week and share a quiet chat. Like Dave Scott, Mark Allen holds iconic status in our sport. When they talk, you should listen. I spoke with Mark about how he used to deal with all of the pressures and stress of race week. I always feel very calm after talking to him.

NEWTON SIGNING AT RACE EXPO //

Race week is high octane.
The town of Kona is buzzing,
and there are triathletes everywhere.

The little training that I do in race week, I like to get done early.
Any intensity that I incorporate is at race pace, but of short duration.
I don't want to fatigue the body, but obviously I don't want to shut
the motor down completely for a week or two leading into a big race.
It's a fine balance. With experience you learn to finesse that balance.
Like a lot of things—for example, nutrition—there is a plan in place,
but within that there is also flexibility.

These sessions can be as much for your head as for your body,
and it's important to recognize this. I rely a lot on internal feedback.
When you've done it enough times, you remember how it felt
when you had great results in the past. At the same time, that last
week or two can take a few different forms and still lead to a
positive performance.

On the Wednesday before race day Julie Dibens and I made our way through the crowds at Dig Me Beach to swim 1.2 miles. We regrouped with Mat Steinmetz at the car park of the nearby Kona Aquatic Center. After a quick change, we were straight out on the bikes. We rode the Queen K for about 90 minutes and did 10 minutes' worth of race-pace effort on the way back into town. Our ride finished at the top of the Energy Lab, where we made another quick change and finished off the day's training with an easy 20-minute jog.

Julie is from Boulder, and, like me, she was working with Mat at the time. We had trained together in Boulder quite a bit over the summer. In race week a lot of decisions are made based on logistics and convenience.

I'm not superstitious, but in the days leading up to a race I read through my training log.

It's a fairly accurate account of my training for the year. I really just record the specifics of the session, not subjective feelings about the training. In my opinion, there's no such thing as a bad session once it's done. Many years ago Neri suggested that I do this for positive affirmation, and it is a pre-race ritual that's stuck with me ever since.

Having known me for 20 years, Neri knows how I tick. It's human nature to have doubts, but you want to control them and not let them take over. So getting positive thoughts in the forefront of your mind is key.

It's satisfying to read the amount of work that has gone into the buildup. Among all the white noise in the days and hours leading up to a race, it's easy to forget the months of training, the countless sessions.

There is also a flip side to this exercise—if you haven't done the work, you are going to read about it. But I have honestly never had that experience.

I read the training log on race morning. It was last thing I did before I left the hotel room.

STRAIGHT AFTER BIKE CHECK-IN
we headed to the Kona Aquatic Center
for the final part of the pre-race-day
warm-up: an easy 10-minute swim with
the crew, Mat Steinmetz and Julie Dibens.

D-day: 4:30 a.m., race morning. It's a combination of a hundred different feelings.

Intense nervousness can be replaced by great excitement in a fleeting moment because of the opportunity that awaits. My mind is racing but is very calm all at the same time.

There is an amazing energy when you get down to the race venue. I feed off the atmosphere at the pier on race morning—I love it. Everyone is excited. It's like Christmas morning before you've unwrapped your presents. No one has had a chance to be disappointed yet.

Then the reality check comes. There are several race-morning formalities to attend to. This year I got to wear the famed number 1 on my arm. With the introduction of the Kona Points Ranking system (KPR) the allocation of race numbers was a little different this year. In the past your KPR reflected your finish from the previous year. Having won in Las Vegas at the 70.3 world championship, I jumped to the lead in the ranking system. It's the third year in a row I've worn race number 1.

As the competitors congregate behind the start line, time seems to stand still.

It can feel like the loneliest place in the world before the start, but you begin to remember your family and friends, all of the people who have pitched in to help you get to that point, all of the people who are going to be watching.

And then the cannon goes off and suddenly frees you from all of the nervousness and apprehension. It's time to put thoughts and plans into action. It's a nice feeling to be finally under way . . . until you get kicked in the head for the first time.

11:30 A.M.

1:10 P.M.

The 120-kilometer (75-mile) mark on the bike: Just one year ago this was the point in the race where it was all slipping away from me.

Twelve months on, it's the polar opposite. On the face of it, this just looks like the lead pack on the Kona course, but to me it's more than that. It represents 12 months of refocusing, planning, and working hard.

In 2010 I was two and a half minutes behind the lead group at this point, dealing with a very different dynamic. The lead group had clearly conspired to work together. That was the beginning of the end. I lost another minute every 10 kilometers and got off the bike nearly eight minutes behind the contenders. I was the defending champion, and as such you are the loneliest person out there. You don't expect any help, and you certainly don't get it.

1:22 P.M. / 16 MILES //

Macca was behind the strategy. He rolled out a blueprint on how to get some of the stronger runners unstuck. It's an individual sport, so we had never really seen this dynamic before on this scale—partnerships of convenience forming.

What happened in 2010 hurt but was good for me. I had to change my strategy, and it made me a better athlete. In years past I would swim with the front group, mark the main contenders on the bike, and wait for the run. This year I was more proactive on the bike; I was determined not to just wait for the other guys to make a move. I was going to make some of the moves myself.

It was a mental shift to be more aggressive and race like a past champion. I was serious about my commitment to improve, in every detail. It wasn't just about the bike but about everything—training, strategy, equipment, and mentality.

The fruits of the last 12 months were evident in this moment. I was at the front of the race and pushing forward rather than slipping away. Chris Lieto is the best cyclist in triathlon. He led off the bike. I was equal second off the bike with Luke McKenzie and Marino Vanhoenacker.

It's a fine line between a great performance
and overstepping the mark, jeopardizing your finish.

MY ENTOURAGE waits at
the finish line. My mum, Neri,
Lucy, Austin, and a good mate,
John, all watch the late race
action unfold on the big screen
(opposite, left and right).

I remember passing Lieto at 8 kilometers (5 miles) into the marathon and thinking, "This is the earliest I've ever been in the lead."

I just tried to stay focused on remaining relaxed, maintaining an efficient technique, and ensuring my nutrition. I was running from the front for the majority of the marathon. I am used to stealing the lead much later. It's a different mentality, leading.

I wasn't running fast toward the end of the race, but I knew I had a substantial lead. I was fighting leg cramps for the last 30 minutes. I even stopped to stretch them out a few times toward the finish.

And then I hit Ali'i Drive. Over the buzz of the crowd I could hear the commentator, Mike Riley, say that I could still break the record. I picked up the speed again. I thought it would be criminal to miss it by a second, so for those last 150 meters I really tried to bring it home.

That brought on the cramping again at the finish line.

It's a fine line between a great performance and overstepping the mark, jeopardizing your finish. It helps that the atmosphere in town is electric, and I tried to let that energy carry me in the last mile, running to an unbelievable finish time.

There is instant relief and excitement in the moment that the dream is realized.

I accomplished my dream of winning the half-Ironman and Ironman world championship double. It was a deeply satisfying victory because I had won in a different way. I had shown another dimension to my racing. Big changes carry big risks but also the possibility of big rewards.

By winning Kona in 2011 I became the oldest men's champion at age 38, the fourth man in history to win three or more (joining Dave Scott, Mark Allen, and Peter Reid), and the first person to win both the half-Ironman and Ironman world championships in the same year.

In the end, the record means less to me than my performance. Sure, it's flattering to have the Kona course record, but it's too hard to compare performances across races and conditions from one year to the next. That's the beautiful thing about the sport. I've been to Kona five times now, and every year brings something different.

As I approached the finish line, my first thought was to acknowledge someone who played a pivotal role in my development as an athlete. My celebration was a tribute to Greg Welch. He won here in 1994, the first Australian to do so, and this was how he crossed the line, although I think he got a little more elevation than I did.

Seeing Mark Allen and Dave Scott waiting to congratulate me when I walked off the ramp was a great personal moment.

They were embracing me, supporting me. Both men are legends in our sport, having won Kona six times. Mark and Dave have been inspirational to me from early on. When I was watching the Ironman world championships on television during the 1980s, it was always those two athletes going head-to-head in the lava fields. They put the sport of triathlon on the map and took it to a wider audience.

I've had various levels of contact with them both over the years, particularly Dave. But this was different. I felt at this moment like I was being accepted, and it felt good. It was an unspoken thing, almost as if I had their approval as an athlete, and that meant a lot.

MY GOOD FRIEND JOHN MINTO draped the Australian flag around me as Greg Welch led me to be interviewed. John and I met nearly 20 years ago at university and formed a lasting friendship. We were groomsmen for each other's weddings. Our friendship was forged in the university gym long before triathlon was even in the picture—John was a professional footballer. He has had a massive influence on my life.

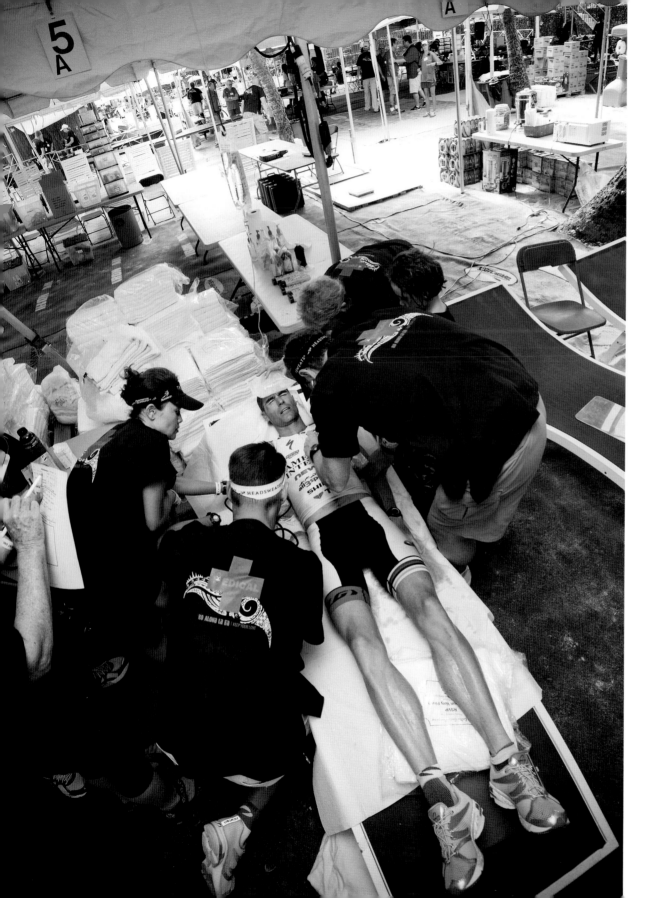

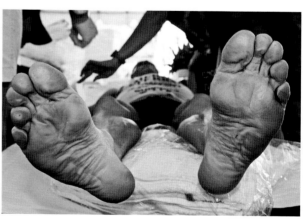

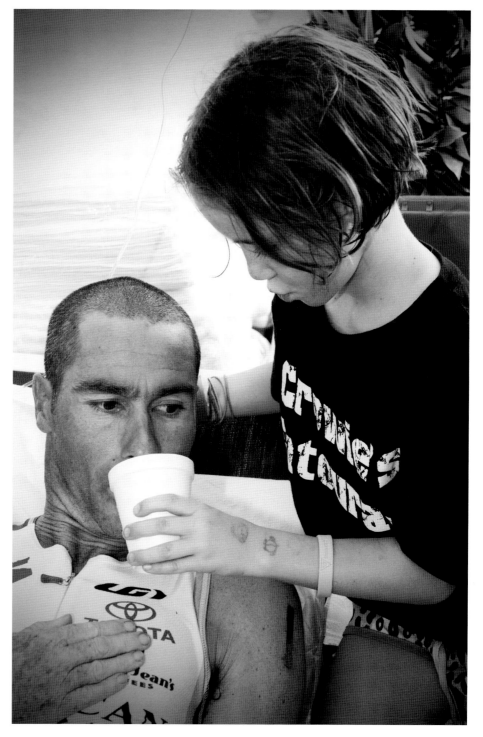

Every year it's not until about five minutes after I finish the race that the physical impact of the effort hits me.

All I want to do is lie down. But the pain is overshadowed by an unprecedented satisfaction and elation.

The pressure is off; I've got the result I wanted. Lying in that medical tent, I look like I'm in rough shape, but I'm absolutely euphoric. It's over. It's not just the end of the race, it's the end of a really long year. Even through the year's setbacks, the goal remained the same, and now I'm finally on the other side. I am the Ironman 70.3 and Ironman world champion.

A QUICK DEBRIEF with friend
and manager Franko Vatterott.

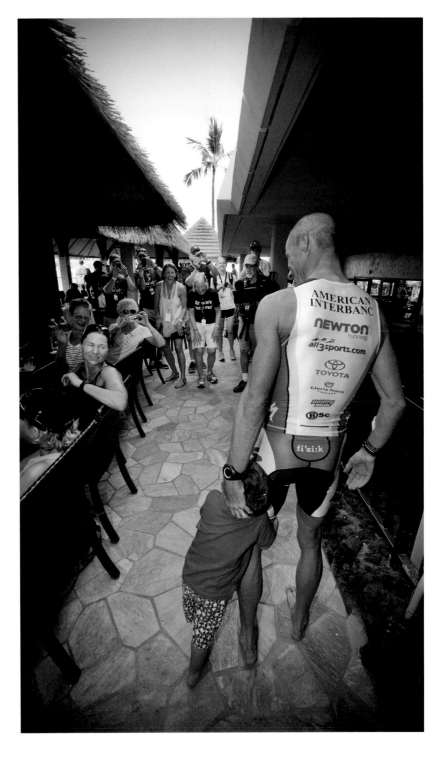

CELEBRATING WITH THE KIDS and family brings me a lot of joy. All the people who made the trip over to watch me race got to see me win. I am always trying to repay the sacrifices my family has made over the years for this career by holding up my end of the deal on race day. I don't have to win for it to be worthwhile, but I did all that I could, and it was my day. All those little things, they mean more than you think.

IT'S A SPECIAL MOMENT when you see Linda Jane Kelley (the official race organizer) coming to size you up for the winner's ring just before the press conference. She and Neri suggested that I have this year's ring made a little larger, so hopefully it will fit after my racing days are over.

WELCHY HOSTS the official press conference. They always have beer and pizza for you—nice post-race food. After fueling your body with gels and sweet electrolyte drinks all day, it's nice to have something a little savory.

AFTER THE PRESS CONFERENCE
we go to the transition area to pick up
my gear and head back to the hotel.
As at the end of any day's work, you
pick up your tools and head home.

MARK COTE is an aerodynamics engineer and product developer for Specialized, and he played a big role in the design of the new Shiv. I have really enjoyed working with such a progressive company that continues to push the boundaries (left).

MY POST-RACE ITINERARY included stops at the Australian athlete recovery breakfast (above), the Oakley party (opposite left), and the TYR house (opposite right) for celebrations and various media commitments.

In the days following the race, I know I will be off-the-charts busy.

I've delivered the victory, and I am happy for my sponsors to take full advantage and capitalize on that. It's nice to repay the faith and support they've shown in us. The Australian athlete recovery breakfast at the Royal Kona Hotel has become somewhat of a ritual. I have spoken here three times now.

Hosted by Cuan Peterson, Welchy, and the Oakley marketing group, the Oakley party is a chance for the athletes to swap stories, jump into an ice bath, or have breakfast prepared by the on-site chef. It's a fun, light-hearted atmosphere after the stress of the preceding weeks. Oakley presents a special gift to the winners, a nice little fringe benefit. In past years the gift has been an engraved watch or limited-edition sunglasses.

The next stop was the TYR house for their post-race get-together. I was on to beer and pizza and it wasn't even lunchtime.

GARY SHIELDS is my masseur in Kona. I see him on a daily basis for a massage, and he also takes me out motorpacing. Over time we have become good friends. Gary is a very good athlete in his own right, having won the Ultraman world championship three times (1988, 1989, and 1990). He still rides his bike competitively. Having been involved with Ironman Hawaii for roughly 30 years as athlete, volunteer, or spectator, Gary has a wealth of knowledge about the race. He's a great ally (right).

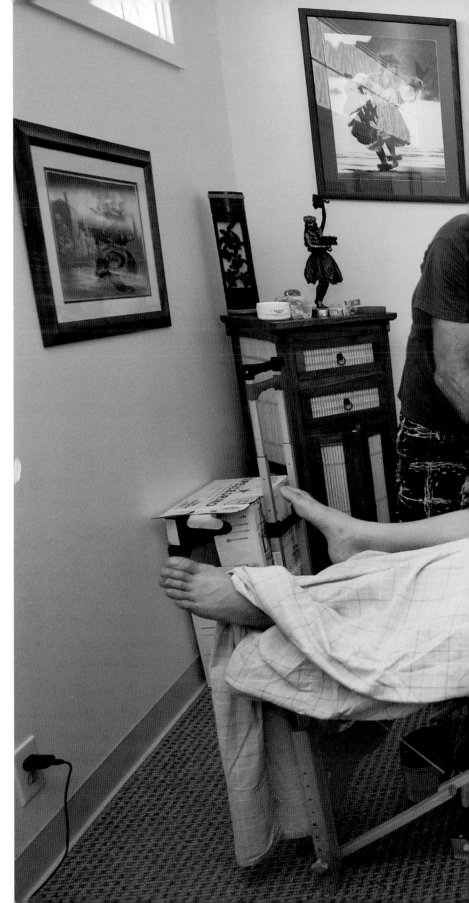

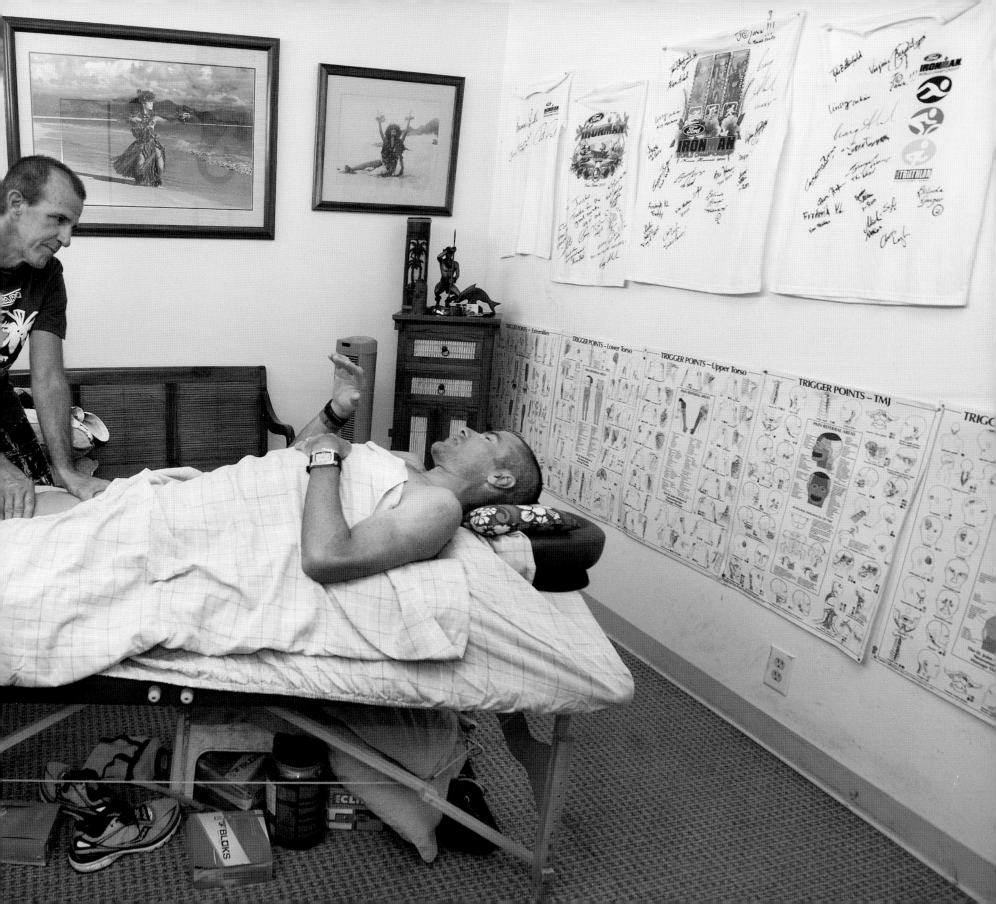

The awards night is a big, spectacular outdoor event that includes highlights on the big screen along with local music and performances.

As the winner, I had the honor of making a victory speech. Each year I've won the race, Chrissie Wellington has as well. I felt pressure to prepare something this year because in the past Chrissie's speeches have been so articulate; she's a tough act to follow.

This race is steeped in tradition from start to finish—the custodians of the land bless the race and say a prayer on its completion at midnight. The leis and trophies that are given to the race winners are a reflection of the Hawaiian culture as well.

A symbol of dedication, emotion, and strength, the 'Umeke bowl is a unique trophy that carries historical and cultural significance in Hawaii. Traditionally, the 'Umeke was used for holding water. Now Hawaiian families often use it to hold sacred things. To receive a gift of such a standard designates honor, accomplishment, fulfillment, completion.

CELEBRATING WITH Chrissie Wellington, who
is now a four-time Kona champion (left). Mike Sinyard
and Bobby Behan from Specialized were two of our
guests at the winner's table (above).

I HAPPENED TO SEE Dave Scott (opposite) and his son Drew on their way to the airport. Drew competed in the race for the first time. Two days after the race, *Outside* magazine did a photo shoot at Dig Me Beach. It's flattering when triathlon is highlighted in a mainstream media publication (above, center, and right).

BRINGING IT HOME Where it all started

I met Neri on a beach on the north coast of New South Wales. It was December 1990, and we were both there with our families on summer holiday, me from Sydney and her from a country town called Tamworth. I was sulking because I didn't have my surfboard since we couldn't fit it in the car. Neri got one of her girlfriends to come and ask me if I wanted to play beach volleyball. We hit it off straightaway, and I spent a lot of time with Neri in the days that followed. I had known her for about a week when I took her home to meet my mum and stepdad. Once Neri had left I remember my mum saying, "Oh, Craig, she's very nice." Like all holidays, it eventually came to an end, and it was time to go home.

I was going into my first year of university, and Neri was beginning her final year of high school. We lived six hours apart by car, but we stayed in contact over the next year, mostly by telephone. Following her graduation from high school, Neri spent a year in London working as a nanny. She was a very good correspondent, me not so much, but we kept up with each other through letters. I had never even considered doing a triathlon at this point. I was aware of the sport, and I liked it, but I was still playing soccer and fumbling around changing university degrees.

In 1994 Neri came to Sydney to study to be a nurse. After a few near misses, I invited her to my 21st birthday party on June 25, 1994. At this point I was just getting into triathlon. I wasn't sure what the sport held for me.

In November 1996, I did a world cup race in Auckland, New Zealand, and finished fourth. At that race I met some other athletes and coaches who were based in France. I received an invitation to race for a club in France the following season, which was 1997. As fate would have it, I graduated in April 1997 and Neri soon thereafter, so we decided it would be an adventure we would undertake together. It seemed like the logical thing to do in terms of the progression of my career, and it would also be fun to live in another country with my girlfriend for five months.

Shortly after we returned to Australia after our second season in France, in 1998, we bought our first apartment in Cronulla, a suburb on the southern outskirts of Sydney. It was the ideal location since Neri got a job as an emergency nurse at St. George Hospital and I was already driving down that way to train most days.

The Hamilton Island Triathlon is a destination race. Neri and I took this opportunity to go on holiday without the kids. We each participated in the race as part of a team.

We are rarely without Lucy and Austin, especially when we are in the United States and our family is not around to help out. For Neri, our six months away are very demanding. She's on call 24/7 as

Mum and business manager as well as handling a million other things that make up her day. That was why this was such a nice break; it was just the two of us.

In 1998 for triathlon in Australia, on the men's side of things you had the big three: Greg Welch, Brad Bevan, and Miles Stewart. Between them they had won pretty much everything in the sport. They were the first tier. There was also an established second level of athletes, and then there were the rest of us.

Triathlon was going to be included in the 2000 Sydney Olympics, and it was very hard for me to get world cup starts, and even harder to get any funding from the governing body of the sport. I was well down in the pecking order. The high-performance managers at the time were aware of me, but I didn't factor into their planning. They made it clear that I had never been a junior athlete, so they hadn't invested in me, and they weren't going to start now.

What I really needed at the time was advice and coaching. I had been in the sport five minutes, and I was pulling training sessions out of triathlon magazines.

The Australian system was set up to pick a competitive Olympic team and win medals. I was never bitter about it—I understood, but I was occasionally frustrated at the lack of opportunities for international racing. As a competitor, you want to race a lot, and you want to be able to pick your races so you can prepare for them. I knew I had potential.

When I did get a world cup start, I had to fund it myself. I relied heavily on Neri during this time. She would often work double shifts to make the mortgage payments and help pay for my travel to races.

Just as my triathlon career was getting well under way, Neri and I were married on January 30, 1999, in Cronulla.

WHEN WE GET HOME FROM KONA, there are many more media commitments, which is great exposure for the sport of triathlon and for me personally. I was asked to fire the start gun for the Run for Fun at Sydney Olympic Park.

I BUMPED INTO MILES STEWART at the Hamilton Island Triathlon.
When I first started in triathlon, Miles Stewart was part of a big squad that
was run by his dad and based on the Gold Coast. Many years ago I did
a couple of training stints with Miles and found that he was always honest
and a good sounding board (above). I teamed up with Karen Handy, wife
of one of the race officials, to do the swim and run legs in Hamilton (right).

NERI AND I enjoyed some activities after Kona that I would not normally get to do during the season because I wouldn't have the time or the energy.

AUSTIN LOVES to get every single toy off the shelf. When we get home in October, there is a lot of play time for Daddy and Aussie.

I am a family guy. To me, it seems totally normal to integrate my family into my profession whenever possible.

I would be riddled with guilt if Neri had to deal with everything on her own or if I missed out on seeing my kids reach major milestones. I can't bear for Lucy or Austin to think that anything I'm doing is more important to me than them. I want us to stay together as a family.

Triathlon doesn't offer as much money as many other major sports, and it is very expensive to travel with your family. I don't judge anyone else for doing it differently, but I wouldn't want it any other way.

When I am overseas it's all work, and when I am in Hawaii it's work, so when I get home I want to stay home. I want to walk Lucy to school; I want to spend time with Austin. I feel like an estranged dad during the last four weeks in Hawaii because it's so busy.

FOR A WHILE NOW, Lucy has
been old enough to ride her bike
alongside me on my recovery runs.
Austin is just starting to join us.
He hasn't got Lucy's endurance yet,
so we normally start the run with a
little circuit so we can loop back past
the car and drop Austin off to Mum
before Lucy and I head out again.

When I started in the sport of triathlon I was living in the Ashfield area, where I grew up. Ashfield Cycles was the first bike shop that I ever walked into.

I struck up a friendship with the owner, John Michell. Knowing that I was a university student, he would always give me a great deal and help me out where he could. I bought my first real racing bike from John.

In 1997 I decided to do my first long-distance race, the New South Wales Half Ironman Championships. Just days before the race, my bike was stolen. I didn't know what to do, so I called John, desperate for a solution. He knew about the race on Sunday, and he told me to come up to his store immediately. John gave me a bike off the rack, no questions asked. When I told him I couldn't afford it, he said we would work that out later. I went on to win the race, and that win really whetted my appetite for half-Ironman and long-distance racing.

When we moved to Cronulla the following year, I lost contact with John. A decade later he called me out of the blue to invite me to the opening of his new concept store. John was changing things up after nearly 40 years in the bike industry. Ironically, he had decided to partner with Specialized, my new bike sponsor. It's interesting the way things turn out.

It was fun to hang out at Ashfield Cycles. My brother Brett and his family still live locally, so they came along. Lucy and I were able to enjoy a cuddle with baby Zaine.

In the off-season I enjoy taking some time to support charitable causes.

I was approached several years ago to be an ambassador for the KIDS Foundation. Susie O'Neill, the founder, established the charity to educate and raise awareness about childhood injury prevention and to raise funds for children with life-changing injuries. Susie and her family are all triathletes, and the KIDS Foundation has been the official charity of Ironman Australia for nearly a decade. It's an honor to represent the KIDS Foundation, and I feel a huge responsibility to be available as the charity's ambassador. It's a humbling experience—these kids are absolutely inspirational, as are the people behind the scenes who do most of the fund-raising work.

One of my partners, Gloria Jean's (a franchised coffeehouse in Australia), is a longtime supporter of Variety, another children's charity in Australia. Gloria Jean's asked me to help promote Variety's annual Santa Fun Run. That's me in the back on prime-time news television. The suits arrived late, and I didn't have time to put on my Santa pants. That's live television for you.

MAT STEINMETZ helps me with most aspects of my triathlon performance: bike fit, planning and scheduling training, and maximizing equipment choices (opposite).

SUB 8 The road ahead

The 2011 season is history. A new race season presents a range of new opportunities. Because of my busy schedule, I decided the first stop of 2012 would be the inaugural running of the Melbourne Ironman at the end of March. It was a marquee race and a regional championship.

This was a little later than I traditionally start racing. Normally I would begin racing in February or early March, but I just didn't feel I would have laid down the required fitness by then. Melbourne would provide me with the opportunity to validate for Kona early in the year, but I was a little apprehensive on two levels.

My first race since Kona would be another Ironman, and I normally like to do a shorter race before an Ironman. This would be the eighth Ironman race of my career and the first time I'd done two consecutively. It was more a mental hurdle than a physical one.

Second, I was stepping straight into a top-shelf field early in the season. Because of the way this race had been positioned as a regional championship with extra dollars and Kona ranking points on offer, a world-class field had been assembled—one truly worthy of Melbourne's status as the Asia-Pacific championship race.

The way the sport and the qualification process for Kona are structured, you really have to plan a season carefully. When you choose to add longer races to a schedule, in my opinion you are more constrained in how often you can race. There are also implications for the longevity of a career.

Personally, I put a positive spin on everything. In the case of Melbourne, I would get to stay home longer, Lucy could stay in school longer, and I would get to scratch that competitive itch in a big race on home soil.

ONE WEEK OUT from the Melbourne Ironman: Motorpace sessions simulate race intensity. I incorporated these sessions into my training regimen about five years ago when I stepped up to the Ironman distance. It's a convenient way to do sustained threshold workouts. There are great fitness adaptations from these sessions. When I'm in Boulder, Mat Steinmetz drives the scooter for me. The skill of the driver makes or breaks the session.

ENDEAVOUR CYCLES: George Poulos has offered me technical advice, service, and support since we moved to Cronulla in 1998 (left).

ENDURO BEARINGS customized the bottom bracket of my new racing bike by engraving my Kona record-breaking time (opposite left).

TROY GLENNAN FROM SHIMANO gave my bike the once-over two days prior to Ironman Melbourne. Shimano's Australia headquarters are very close to our house, so I receive amazing support (opposite right).

Early in my career, I remember many of the best athletes at the time telling me that the hallmark of a great career is the ability to perform consistently, and also to be versatile as an athlete.

It's not possible to win every time you race, but you can prepare to bring a consistently high level of performance to every race and to each discipline within the race.

I made it my mission to be versatile and to be a factor on any course—hilly, flat, windy, hot, cold, short, medium, or long. I've always admired athletes in other sports who are good across the board. The greatest tennis players can adapt their game to any surface, and the greatest golfers can do likewise, regardless of the style of course they are playing. I wanted to be the kind of triathlete that would fit that mold.

I've been pigeonholed as a runner. If you win a lot of races, particularly if you take the lead during the run, I think it's inevitable that this will happen. Triathlons have always finished with the run discipline. But triathlon is not just running.

People who know the sport intimately will tell you that your final outcome is always determined by how you put the three disciplines together. During a race, the way you swim undeniably affects the way you ride. Likewise, the way you do both of these affects how you run. It's the combination of the three disciplines that defines the uniqueness of our sport. To win major races and be consistent, you can't have any weaknesses.

EVEN IN TRANSITION it's hard to escape the cameras on race morning.

ONE LAST INTERVIEW with the host TV broadcaster before the gun goes off (above).
The introductions are the final formality before we hit the water. I was last in, wearing race
number 1 (right).

RIDING THROUGH THE TUNNEL on the bike course on the EastLink Tollway was a unique experience.

I had a slow start to the race. I missed the lead swim group by over 3 minutes, the guys I would normally come out of the water with.

I didn't panic, but I was disappointed because swimming was the one thing I'd done consistently well in training all summer. In a moment like this you have to acknowledge that you haven't given yourself the ideal start, but it's a long race, and it's far from over.

I was able to ride back into contention. I felt very comfortable physically, albeit a little cold, and after finding my way to the front I was getting great feedback from my legs. An epic duel with Cameron Brown ensued in the marathon.

THE EMBRYONIC STAGES of my duel with Cameron Brown began in the early kilometers of the marathon. Joe Gambles was also in our group here.

TWO OF MY biggest supporters, Mat and Franko, celebrating post-race. They had made the trip from Boulder. I really appreciate the level of support I get from my team (left). There to greet me at the finish was none other than my biggest fan, the adorable Lucy Mia (opposite).

I broke the tape at the inaugural Asia-Pacific Championship in Melbourne, in 7:57:44. It was my first time under 8 hours and my eighth Ironman.

To be brutally honest, I was more happy with the performance than with the time. Times are so dependent on conditions and courses and can be akin to comparing apples to oranges in many situations. In our sport, how do you cancel out all of the variables—time of year, weather, competition, and so on? How do you rank a performance on a course that is cool and flat compared with one that is hot and hilly? As far as I'm concerned, times mean little. They are just another talking point. What's important is your level of performance.

For me, this was more about beating a world-class field on home soil, knowing that I managed to beat people who were in good form. The media were reporting that it was one of the best fields assembled outside Kona.

It was announced just before the race that the men's and women's trophies would be named after Australian triathlon royalty: Greg Welch and Michellie Jones.

I really wanted mine to be the first name on Greg's trophy. As in Kona, I was motivated by the desire to make my race a tribute to one of the athletes whom I most admire. It was a personally satisfying victory.

In 1995, while still at university, I was contacted by Triathlon New South Wales, the governing body of the sport in our state. A TV commercial was being filmed, and they were looking for some extras. The star of the commercial was Greg Welch, winner of the Ironman World Championship the previous year. The extras ended up being Simon Whitfield, who went on to become our sport's first Olympic gold medalist; Greg Bennett, another of triathlon's most decorated athletes; and me.

We changed locations many times throughout the course of the two days. I would always position myself in a car with Welchy and bombard him with question after question. He was gracious to a fault and answered every one of my questions, even the ridiculous ones. I learned so much about the sport of triathlon that day, but the most important thing I learned is that being a great champion starts after you've crossed the finish line.

Greg has always been a big inspiration within the sport. I often wonder what would have happened if he hadn't taken so much time with a 21-year-old kid who had been in the sport for five minutes.

I have known and raced Brownie for over a decade. He's one of the gentlemen of the sport and a true legend. His résumé includes four podium finishes in Hawaii, a European championship, and an unprecedented 10 Ironman New Zealand titles—a record I think will never be broken.

Epilogue

This book is a *real* reflection of twelve months of our lives and the years that brought us to this point. What began as the preparation and buildup to two major championship races came to include all of the challenges that accompany professional racing—sponsorship, illness, injury, and family life. Paul Robbins traveled with us extensively to capture the behind-the-scenes moments. We aimed to tell the story, in words and images, of what it takes both physically and mentally to race at this level.

As a professional athlete, I have continually tried to share my passion, perseverance, dedication, and work ethic. It goes without saying that years spent pursuing any goal so single-mindedly exact a toll on mind, body, and relationships. At the end of the season I stop to evaluate whether I can sustain this level of commitment for another year because I don't think there is another way to compete. I'm not the sort of person who can live with regrets.

I'm serious about my sport, but ultimately I hope this book conveys a sense of fun too. I am playing sport for a living, doing what I love to do, fulfilling a childhood dream and getting to share it with my family. I'm not an emergency nurse saving lives; I'm a professional athlete: I get paid to do what I love to do and what I would do for nothing. It's a unique opportunity that binds us together as a family, living away from home for half the year, every year. It's an adventure.

I have no regrets. I'm wholeheartedly thankful for the help and support I have received. My story began with the idea that I could succeed as a professional athlete. It was a massive risk, but I believed I could do it.

Whether you compete for fun or for the podium, it's my hope that you persevere and do the same. Believe in yourself.

ture National Triathlon Series Australian Long-Course Championship Australian Sprint Distance Championship Boulder Peak Triathlon California Half-Ironman Escape from Alcatraz 5430 Long Course Triathlon Forster Half-Ironman Ironman Coeur d'Alene Ironman Melbourne Ironman Port Macquarie Ironman World Championship Ironman 70.3 Boise

ACHIEVEMENTS Ironman 70.3 California Ironman 70.3 Florida Ironman 70.3 Geelong Ironman 70.3 Honu Ironman 70.3 Kansas Ironman 70.3 Muskoka Ironman 70.3 Newfoundland Iron-man 70.3 Racine Ironman 70.3 Singapore Ironman 70.3 St. Croix Ironman 70.3 Vineman Ironman 70.3 World Championship ITU Continental Cup Boston ITU International Points Race Mazatlan ITU World Cup Edmonton ITU World Cup Geelong ITU World Cup Ishigaki ITU World Cup Mooloolaba ITU World Cup St. Petersburg ITU World Cup Tiszaujvaros ITU World Cup Championship Laguna Phuket Triathlon Life Time Fitness Triathlon Los Angeles Triathlon Mrs. T's Chicago Triathlon Newport Beach Triathlon New York City Triathlon Noosa Triathlon Pacific Coast ITU International Points Race Pacific Coast Sprint Triathlon Pacific Grove Triathlon Philadelphia Triathlon Port of Tauanga Half-Ironman Ralph's Half-Ironman California REV3 Triathlon San Diego Triathlon Classic Spirit of Racing Half-Ironman

2012

1st / Ironman Melbourne (Asia-Pacific Championship) / Australia // 7:57:44

1st / Ironman 70.3 EagleMan / Cambridge, MD // 3:44:57

2011

6th / Abu Dhabi International Triathlon / United Arab Emirates // 6:46:46

13th / Escape from Alcatraz / San Francisco, CA // 2:09:28

1st / Ironman Coeur d'Alene / ID // 8:19:48

8th / Ironman 70.3 Racine / WI // 4:09:52

1st / Ironman 70.3 World Championship / Las Vegas, NV // 3:54:48

1st / Ironman World Championship / Kona, HI // 8:03:56

2010

1st / Ironman 70.3 Geelong / Victoria // 3:53:15

1st / Australian Long-Course Championship / Huskisson, New South Wales // 3:36:04

1st / Ironman 70.3 Singapore // 3:53:31

3rd / St. Anthony's Triathlon / St. Petersburg, FL // 1:49:14

DNF / Ironman 70.3 St. Croix / U.S. Virgin Islands //

1st / REV3 Triathlon / Middlebury, CT // 3:59:20

1st / Ironman 70.3 Boise / ID // 4:02:11

3rd / Life Time Fitness Triathlon / Minneapolis, MN // 1:49:45

1st / Ironman 70.3 Racine / WI // 3:48:56

1st / Ironman 70.3 Muskoka / Ontario // 3:58:33

4th / Ironman World Championship / Kona, HI // 8:16:53

2009

1st / Ironman 70.3 Geelong / Victoria // 3:50:51

2nd / Australian Long-Course Championship / Huskisson, New South Wales // 3:51:06

1st / Ironman 70.3 Singapore // 3:47:34

1st / Ironman 70.3 Honu / HI // 4:02:52

1st / Ironman 70.3 Boise / ID // 3:51:46

5th / Life Time Fitness Triathlon / Minneapolis, MN // 1:51:56

8th / Ironman 70.3 Vineman / Sonoma County, CA // 4:05:59

1st / Ironman 70.3 Muskoka / Ontario // 3:58:04

1st / Ironman World Championship / Kona, HI // 8:20:21

2008

2nd / Ironman 70.3 California / Oceanside // 3:58:25

4th / St. Anthony's Triathlon / St. Petersburg, FL // 1:49:41

1st / Ironman 70.3 St. Croix / U.S. Virgin Islands // 4:05:34

DNF / Ironman 70.3 Florida / Orlando //

3rd / Escape from Alcatraz / San Francisco, CA // 2:02:53

2nd / Ironman 70.3 Kansas / Lawrence // 3:59:59

8th / Life Time Fitness Triathlon / Minneapolis, MN // 1:49:34

2nd / Ironman 70.3 Vineman / Sonoma County, CA // 3:51:25

1st / Ironman 70.3 Newfoundland / Corner Brook // 3:59:45

1st / Ironman 70.3 Muskoka / Ontario // 4:10:31

1st / Ironman World Championship / Kona, HI // 8:17:45

2007

1st / Australian Long-Course Championship / Huskisson, New South Wales // 3:36:53

3rd / Ironman Port Macquarie / New South Wales // 8:38:49

3rd / St. Anthony's Triathlon / St. Petersburg, FL // 1:48:07

1st / Ironman 70.3 St. Croix / U.S. Virgin Islands // 4:04:52

1st / Disney Ironman 70.3 Florida / Orlando // 3:50:27

1st / Subaru Muskoka Long-Course Triathlon / Ontario // 2:42:12

1st / Philadelphia Triathlon / PA // 1:52:18

3rd / Life Time Fitness Triathlon / Minneapolis, MN // 1:49:21

1st / Ironman 70.3 Vineman / Sonoma County, CA // 3:50:49

1st / Ironman 70.3 Newfoundland / Corner Brook // 3:58:26

2nd / Ironman World Championship / Kona, HI // 8:19:04

4th / Ironman 70.3 World Championship / Clearwater, FL // 3:44:10

2006

1st / Australian Long-Course Championship / Huskisson, New South Wales // 3:35:25

5th / St. Anthony's Triathlon / St. Petersburg, FL // 1:50:16

6th / Oceania Championships / Geelong, Victoria // 1:52:28

1st / St. Croix Half-Ironman / U.S. Virgin Islands // 4:07:33

13th / Life Time Fitness "Battle of the Sexes" Triathlon / Minneapolis, MN // 1:52:14

2nd / Subaru Muskoka Long-Course Triathlon / Ontario // 2:40:46

3rd / Nautica New York City Triathlon / NY // 1:45:17

1st / Boulder Peak Triathlon / CO // 1:56:18

1st / 5430 Long-Course Triathlon / Boulder, CO // 3:55:16

1st / Accenture Chicago Triathlon / IL // 1:49:54

2nd / Los Angeles Triathlon / CA // 1:48:25

4th / Noosa Triathlon / Queensland // 1:51:21

1st / Ironman 70.3 World Championship / Clearwater, FL // 3:45:37

2nd / ITU World Long-Course Championship / Canberra // 6:00:35

2005

1st / Port of Tauranga Half-Ironman (New Zealand Long-Course Championship) / Mount Maunganui // 3:49:16

1st / Australian Sprint Distance Championship / Coffs Harbour, New South Wales //

2nd / Australian Long-Course Championship / Port Macquarie, New South Wales //

4th / ITU World Cup Triathlon Mooloolaba / Queensland // 1:59:50

4th / ITU World Cup Triathlon / Ishigaki, Japan // 1:47:33

7th / Escape from Alcatraz / San Francisco, CA // 2:08:36

2nd / Subaru Muskoka Long-Course Triathlon / Ontario // 2:38:34

1st / Life Time Fitness "Battle of the Sexes" Triathlon / Minneapolis, MN // 1:59:32

15th / ITU World Cup Edmonton / Alberta // 1:49:51

1st / 5430 Long-Course Triathlon / Boulder, CO // 3:57:01

4th / Accenture Chicago Triathlon / IL // 1:50:29

1st / ITU Continental Cup Boston / MA // 1:42:15

DNF / ITU World Cup Championship / Gamagōri, Japan //

2nd / Laguna Phuket Triathlon / Thailand //

2004

2nd / Accenture National Triathlon Series, Race 2 / St. Kilda, Victoria //

Bronze / Australian Sprint Distance Championship / Geelong, Victoria //

8th / Accenture National Triathlon Series, Race 4 / Perth, Western Australia // 1:54:50

Gold / Australian Long-Course Championship / Port Macquarie, New South Wales //

3rd / Accenture National Triathlon Series, Race 5 / Sydney, New South Wales //

3rd overall / Accenture National Triathlon Series, 2003–2004 //

4th / California Half-Ironman / Oceanside // 4:10:18

4th / St. Anthony's Triathlon / St. Petersburg, FL // 1:51:56

2nd / Accenture National Triathlon Series, Race 2 / St. Kilda, Victoria //

2nd / St. Croix Half-Ironman / U.S. Virgin Islands // 4:14:00

4th / Escape from Alcatraz / San Francisco, CA // 1:57:53

6th / Bellingham ITU American Cup / WA // 2:02:10

2nd / San Diego Triathlon Classic / CA // 1:28:54

7th / Life Time Fitness "Battle of the Sexes" Triathlon / Minneapolis, MN // 1:51:09

1st / Spirit of Racine Half-Ironman / WI // 3:45:30

1st / Accenture Chicago Triathon / IL // 1:52:09

1st / U.S. Pro Championship / Boston, MA // 1:43:09

1st / Los Angeles Triathlon / CA // 1:49:05

2nd / Noosa Triathlon / Queensland // 1:48:01

1st / Laguna Phuket Triathlon / Thailand // 2:33:07

2003

1st / Accenture National Series Race / Canberra //

1st / Australian Long-Course Championship / Port Macquarie, New South Wales //

8th / Accenture National Triathlon Series, Race 2 / Sydney, New South Wales // 0:57:02

6th / Accenture National Triathlon Series, Race 3 / Coffs Harbour, New South Wales // 0:57:48

15th / ITU Oceania Cup / Devonport, Tasmania // 1:55:06

4th / Australian Olympic Distance Triathlon Championship / Mooloolaba, Queensland //

2nd / Accenture National Series Race / St. Kilda, Victoria // 1:47:31

4th overall / Accenture National Triathlon Series 2002–2003 //

12th / ITU World Cup Race / St. Petersburg, FL // 1:46:16

1st / St. Croix Half-Ironman / U.S. Virgin Islands // 4:08:13

5th / Utah Half-Ironman / Provo // 3:59:27

1st / Newport Beach Triathlon / CA //

4th / Escape from Alcatraz / San Francisco, CA // 2:09:55

3rd / San Diego Triathlon Classic / CA //

15th / Life Time Fitness "Battle of the Sexes" Triathlon / Minneapolis, MN //

2nd / Pacific Coast ITU International Points Race / Newport Beach, CA // 1:52:17

3rd / Mrs. T's Chicago Triathlon / IL //

9th / U.S. Pro Championship (ITU Pan American Cup) / Boston, MA // 1:46:15

3rd / Los Angeles Triathlon / CA // 1:55:36

5th / Noosa Triathlon / Queensland // 1:46:27

4th / ITU World Cup Geelong / Victoria // 1:57:37

DNF / Laguna Phuket Triathlon / Thailand //

8th / Accenture National Triathlon Series, Race 1 / Coffs Harbour, New South Wales // 2:08:38

2002

DNF / Australian Sprint Championship / St. Kilda, Victoria //

7th / ITU World Cup Triathlon Geelong / Victoria // 1:52:51

7th / Australian Olympic Distance Championship / Mooloolaba, Queensland //

20th / ITU World Cup Triathlon / St. Petersburg, FL // 1:55:56

8th / St. Croix Half-Ironman / U.S. Virgin Islands // 4:18:46

2nd / Ralph's Half-Ironman California / Oceanside // 3:48:28

5th / Escape from Alcatraz / San Francisco, CA //

1st / ITU International Points Race / Mazatlán, Mexico //

1st / San Diego Triathlon Classic / CA //

1st / Pacific Coast Sprint Triathlon / Newport Beach, CA //

7th / Life Time Fitness "Battle of the Sexes" Triathlon / Minneapolis, MN //

8th / ITU World Cup Tiszaujvaros / Hungary // 1:46:21

3rd / Mrs. T's Chicago Triathlon / IL //

3rd / U.S. Pro Triathlon Championship / Boston, MA //

2nd / Los Angeles Triathlon / CA // 1:50:00

3rd / Pacific Grove Triathlon / Monterey, CA //

2nd / Noosa Triathlon / Queensland // 1:48:57

1st / Forster Half-Ironman / New South Wales //

1st / Laguna Phuket Triathlon / Thailand // 2:32:48

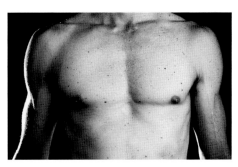

TWO DAYS AFTER MELBOURNE:
Ironman racing exacts a toll on your body
because it's such a long, sustained effort.

Acknowledgments

To Mum for being at all my early races and being my first sponsor. To Jock for instilling in me a love of competitive sport and for waking me at 2 a.m. to watch all of those football games together. I miss you. To Dad and Dorothy, Brett and Nettie, and all of Neri's family for being the best cheer squads and being happy to let Neri and me "do our thing." To our "second families" worldwide who welcome us, our kids, and our luggage and who open up your homes and your hearts. To our friends, too many to mention, thanks for being a part of the journey.

To Welchy, the "plucky" athlete, whom I read about while standing in countless newsagents all over Sydney, thanks for waking in me the thirst to race triathlons. My wingman, John Minto, you are my best mate, best man, sounding board, and voice of reason. To Kev Laws, thanks for squeezing me into your MG and dragging me to running events all over Sydney, and for keeping me real. To Pete Ryan, thanks for helping me buy my first bike, that piece of junk out of the Trading Post. The dream kicked off with that first race in Kurnell. To James Burgess and Gary Emerton, thanks for being my early-day whipping boys. And to Gaz, thanks for having my back at McDonald's when we got ambushed by that carload of guys after we wore a milkshake.

To Greg Rogers, an amazing athlete and coach whom I followed over many years to multiple pools around Sydney. To Wilko, thanks for trying to sort out that left arm of mine. To Christine Gilfeather, my unbelievable massage therapist and friend. You are such an amazing balanced person, sounding board, and brilliant listener. I'm glad you made the trek to Kona. To Pete Coulson for telling me not always what I wanted to hear but always what I needed to hear. For teaching

THANK YOU ■ MUM ■ JOCK ■ DAD ■ DOROTHY ■ BRETT ■ NETTIE ■ NERI'S FAMILY ■ "SECOND FAMILIES" WORLDWIDE ■ OUR FRIENDS ■ WELCHY ■ JOHN MINTO ■ KEV LAWS ■ PETE RYAN ■ JAMES BURGESS ■ GARY EMERTON ■ GAZ ■ GREG ROGERS ■ WILKO ■ CHRISTINE GILFEATHER ■ PETE COULSON ■ FRANKO ■ MAT STEINMETZ ■ KIERAN BARRY ■ JABBA ■ WHITEY ■ LEESY ■ JARRAD ■ BARNEY

me how to be a true professional and for being my friend away from the sport. To Franko Vatterott, my manager, good mate, and roomie for doing all the work I hate to do. To Mat Steinmetz for coming on board and having great attention to detail and meticulous preparation. To Kieran Barry for expressing support when no one else did. To Jabba for letting me sweat it out in your garage a million times, and to my many training partners over the years, including Whitey, Leesy, Jarrad, Barney (aka Spongey), Rinny, Julie Dibens, Jules, Dwight Woodforth, Steve Hackett, Boxhead, Bevan Docherty, Clarky, and Luke McKenzie, and in the early years Simon Whitfield and Greg Bennett. Thanks for making the miles and the years fly by.

To Dave Scott for being a true friend and a great believer, and for navigating my path to Kona.

To my sponsors and supporters, past and present—thanks for being part of my dream and for supporting me to the top of my game. To Carol Oakley, a heartfelt thanks for all the late nights helping me piece together this story, and to Paul for taking the time to capture these amazing images.

To the athletes I have raced who have pushed me to the limit and beyond, thanks for bringing out my best. You are a reflection of your competition.

To my beautiful wife, Neri. For loving and supporting me unconditionally. To Lucy and Austin, thanks for coming along for the ride. It would not have been the same without you to share it with.

—CRAIG ALEXANDER

■ RINNY ■ JULIE DIBENS ■ JULES ■ DWIGHT WOODFORTH ■ STEVE HACKETT ■ BOXHEAD ■ BEVAN DOCHERTY ■ CLARKY ■ LUKE McKENZIE ■ SIMON WHITFIELD ■ GREG BENNETT ■ DAVE SCOTT ■ SPONSORS ■ SUPPORTERS ■ CAROL OAKLEY ■ ATHLETES I HAVE RACED ■ NERI ■ LUCY ■ AUSTIN

My wife, Ludivine, for her unwavering support for and belief in me and this book.

Mum and Dad, for pushing me through the tough times in the beginning, and for letting me transform your laundry into a darkroom all those years ago.

My French family, Sylvie and Poupoune, who have given Ludi and me the world of support and love when we've needed it the most—*gros bisous*.

Craig, Nerida, Lucy, and Austin, I can't thank you enough for allowing me unlimited access into your lives for 18 months. We had a great ride and achieved some amazing things that I'll never forget.

Franko Vatterott, mate, if it wasn't for you I wouldn't be writing this and would never have been able to capture a lot of the images in this book.

Carol Oakley, whom I've worked with a lot and again on this project— it's always great having you on board.

Mat Steinmetz, for all the tip-offs on Craig's movements.

All the assistants and drivers, Dave Baigent, Phillip Baigent, Graham Norris, Greg McCarthy, Steve Bova, Andrew Hunter, John Minto, Gilad Jacobs, Alicia Bockel, Belinda Van Berkel, Elaine Gower, and Tiffany Loftus-Hills on the Jet Ski, thanks for placing me where I needed to be.

THANK YOU ■ LUDIVINE ■ MUM ■ DAD ■ SYLVIE ■ POUPOUNE ■ CRAIG ■ NERI ■ LUCY ■ AUSTIN ■ FRANKO VATTEROTT ■ CAROL OAKLEY ■ MAT STEINMETZ ■ DAVE BAIGENT ■ PHILLIP BAIGENT ■ GRAHAM NORRIS ■ GREG McCARTHY ■ STEVE BOVA ■ ANDREW HUNTER ■ JOHN MINTO ■ GILAD JACOBS ■ ALICIA BOCKEL ■ BELINDA VAN BERKEL ■ ELAINE GOWER ■ TIFFANY LOFTUS-HILLS ■ PAUL DENNETT ■ LISA HANRAHAN ■ DWIGHT WOODFORTH ■ JOHN VEAGE ■ PETER EASTWAY ■ JOHN DUKE ■ SHANE SMITH ■ SHELBY TUTTLE ■ CIARAN HANDY ■ RYAN BOWD ■ STEVE WATSON ■

The advisers to whom I owe a great deal, Paul Dennett and Lisa Hanrahan, Dwight Woodforth, John Veage, and Peter Eastway.

For all the race and location access, a massive thank-you goes to John Duke, Shane Smith, and Shelby Tuttle at WTC; Ciaran Handy at Hamilton Island; Ryan Bowd and Steve Watson at IMG; Shelbi Okumura; and Fiona Melino at Sutherland Shire Leisure Centres.

Industry support, Dustin Brady Shimano USA, Matt Bazzano & Michelle Ferris Shimano Australia, Robert Lindsay Nikon Professional Services Australia, George Poulos Endeavour Cycles, George Gourlas & Andrew Valacas Cronulla Crust, Chuck Panaccione Colorado Multisport, and HPRC Cases Australia.

Our contractors, Narelle Spangher and Georgina Morrison, for covering for me while I was away.

Last but definitely not least, all my triathlon, cycling, and industry friends out there in Australia and across the globe. You have all inspired me in some way or another to produce what I have today. Thank you.

—PAUL K. ROBBINS

SHELBI OKUMURA ▪ FIONA MELINO ▪ DUSTIN BRADY ▪ MATT BAZZANO ▪ MICHELLE FERRIS ▪ ROBERT LINDSAY ▪ GEORGE POULOS ▪ GEORGE GOURLAS ▪ ANDREW VALACAS ▪ CHUCK PANACCIONE ▪ HPRC CASES AUSTRALIA ▪ NARELLE SPANGHER ▪ GEORGINA MORRISON ▪ ALL MY TRIATHLON, CYCLING, AND INDUSTRY FRIENDS IN AUSTRALIA AND ACROSS THE GLOBE

About the photographer

Paul Robbins has been behind the lens all his life and has worked commercially since 1985. His work appears regularly in national magazines and newspapers and can also be seen on billboards, promotional material, and websites.

As a former age-group competitor in triathlons, including Ironman-distance races, Paul is interested in capturing the true beauty of the sport. By shadowing Craig Alexander for over a year, he aimed to capture the passion, craft, and plight of the professional athlete. The opportunity to work without boundaries, without a commercial brief, was a welcome chance to create an original, artistic showcase for the sport.

His other passions are his family, surfing, and bike riding; taking time to smell the roses; and enjoying South Sydney, where he lives with his wife and two children.